Digital Storytelling:

Creating an eStory

Dusti D. Howell
Deanne K. Howell

Linworth
PUBLISHING, INC

Adobe® Photoshop Elements® and Adobe® Premiere® screen shots reprinted with permission from Adobe Systems, Inc. Adobe® Photoshop Elements® and Adobe® Premiere® are registered trademarks of Adobe Systems Incorporated in the United States and other countries.

Kid Pix® Delux 3 screen shots reprinted with permission from Riverdeep, Inc.
Kid Pix Delux 3 © 2000 Riverdeep Interactive Learning Limited. All rights reserved. Used with permission.

Macromedia Flash™ screen shots reprinted with permission from Macromedia, Inc. Macromedia® does not sponsor, affiliate, or endorse this book. Macromedia is a registered trademark of Macromedia, Inc. in the United States and other countries.

Microsoft® PowerPoint® screen shots reprinted by permission from Microsoft Corporation.

Pinnacle® Studio® screen shots reprinted by permission from Pinnacle Systems, Inc.

Library of Congress Cataloging-in-Publication Data

Howell, Dusti.
  Digital storytelling : creating an estory / Dusti D. Howell, Deanne K.
Howell.
     p. cm.
   ISBN 1-58683-080-5 (pbk.)
  1. Interactive multimedia--Handbooks, manuals, etc. 2. Media programs
(Education)--Handbooks, manuals, etc. 3. Authorship--Computer network
resources--Handbooks, manuals, etc. 4. Authorship--Computer
programs--Handbooks, manuals, etc. 5. Computer-assisted
instruction--Handbooks, manuals, etc. I. Howell, Deanne K. II. Title.
   LB1028.55.H68 2003
   371.33'5--dc21

                                2003010521

Published by Linworth Publishing, Inc.
480 East Wilson Bridge Road, Suite L
Worthington, Ohio 43085

Copyright © 2003 by Linworth Publishing, Inc.

ISBN: 1-58683-080-5

5 4 3 2 1

Table of Contents

Acknowledgements

A book like this simply could not have been published without the contribution of a number of dedicated and talented people. We would like to thank the following individuals for their efforts:

Contributing Authors

Dena Wieland did an incredible amount of work in the initial development of the Kid Pix, Studio, and Premiere chapters. Dena helped integrate hundreds of screen captures with simple, straightforward, step-by-step directions for creating basic digital stories with these separate programs.

Dale Rusche helped pioneer digital storytelling at Emporia State University while working on his master's project. His assistance and development in writing the Flash chapter was sorely needed. We are also grateful for his help in editing the Premiere chapter.

Artists

Brad Williams created the images for the "olfactory" animation in the Flash chapter.

Introduction

Background

The authors were first introduced to the finer elements of raconteuring in a graduate course in storytelling. Soon afterwards, they began to collect stories that could be integrated into their classes to facilitate learning. Having taught at every grade level from grade school through graduate school, the collection has continued. In 1999, after attending the *Digital Storytelling Conference & Festival*, the authors began to explore the development of some stories into a digital format. Since that time, they have developed many digital stories for use in national, regional, state, and class presentations.

Purpose and Format of this Book

The purpose of this book is to introduce digital storytelling, a powerful new teaching tool. Benefits and advantages of this type of storytelling will be followed by several tutorials with step-by-step guidance on how to build personal stories in a number of software applications appropriate for use in schools. Tutorial coverage will be limited to a simple story in each of the chapters. A final chapter will discuss methods and ideas for improving the design and development of these stories as well as digital storytelling tips for the presentation of the final productions.

The intended audience is classroom teachers and library media specialists. With more and more computers being integrated into education today, the need and pressure to use the computer in exemplary ways is growing. Teachers can use digital stories to add value to traditional lectures or may even require students to build them for use in portfolios, projects, and presentations.

Content of the Book

Although this book is basically a software tutorial guide, the software selected and the commands given were written for PC (IBM compatible) computers. Although each tutorial is a little different, a multimedia-enabled computer—with speakers, a microphone, a scanner, and FireWire capabilities (all useful hardware components)—is helpful when developing digital stories.

The first chapter introduces the reader to digital storytelling followed by a section that addresses how users may develop or locate digital media, including digital images, sounds, and movie clips. Intellectual property rights and fair-use guidelines are also addressed in this opening chapter. The final chapter gives users tips on how to tell better digital stories and includes thematic designing and presentation options and techniques. An index and two appendixes are included in the book.

The core of the book revolves around developing five different digital stories with five different software packages. Each of the five software chapters includes the following major headings:

1. **Introduction**—A brief explanation of the project, needed materials for the project, and a set of pictures to illustrate the finished project.
2. **Materials Needed**—Exactly what is needed to be able to follow along with this tutorial.
3. **A Look at the Completed Project**—A visual rendition is given for what is being built and what it should look like when finished.
4. **Getting Started with a Storyboard**—A view of what the storyboard might look like before the project begins. In this way, good habits and best practices of the best storytellers can be modeled and showcased. An appendix at the end of the book has examples of blank storyboards available for scanning and reproducing.
5. **Building the Project**—The tutorial begins, complete with screen captures used as a visual aids in this step-by-step approach to creating a digital story.
6. **Adaptations and Extensions**—The first part of this section will include other ideas, which may be simple ideas or interesting software program possibilities that were not covered, to explore in improving the existing story. A second section will extrapolate ideas for how the software and related stories can be used to make other curriculum connections.
7. **Resources**—Sources of online tutorials and extra help for using the software will be given. Also, the sources for stories, software, or digital materials will be cited here at the end of each chapter.
8. **Glossary**—Definitions will be provided for terms that may give readers problems.

Selected Software

Digital stories can be created with a number of software programs, five of which were chosen for use in this book.

1. **Riverdeep's Kid Pix**—An elementary level drawing and art program. This is a very easy program to learn. Kids respond positively to the easy-to-use and creative tools and the sound effects that accompany them. The presentation metaphor in this program lends itself well to telling digital stories.
2. **Pinnacle Studio**—An introductory level digital video-editing program. This award-winning program is very much the PC equivalent to Macintosh's iMovie. It is very easy-to-use and inexpensive, and the finished results are excellent.
3. **Microsoft PowerPoint**—A presentation program. This is the top-selling presentation program in the world and the leading software choice for corporations developing demonstration materials. It is also growing in popularity in schools around the world. In some schools, students in third grade are required to develop presentations with PowerPoint.
4. **Adobe Premiere**—An advanced digital video-editing program. This is the classic favorite of hard-core digital storytellers. It has been taught in the past at the *Digital Storytelling Festival's Boot Camp*. This high-end program is one of the more complex programs covered in this book. However, the level

of quality this program can generate is consistent with the best documentaries shown on television.

5. **Macromedia Flash** — A Web-authoring program. This is a popular storytelling tool for online development of cartoon-style stories. The free Flash player comes preinstalled on most computer browsers today and is on over 98% of all Internet-enabled computers. Adobe LiveMotion can also be used to create Flash files. Some Web developers claim that it is much more user-friendly than Flash. We chose Flash because it is currently the more popular of the two programs.

Editing graphics for use in these stories often requires the use of an additional software program. Appendix B, at the end of the book, features tutorials for image editing using Adobe Photoshop Elements. This program is fantastic for schools and media labs as it is reasonably priced and has many of the features of the full version of Photoshop. Everything needed to complete the stories in this book can easily be accomplished with Photoshop Elements.

Use of the Book

The step-by-step tutorial approach to learning software, or to improving one's ability to use software, is one of the more popular ways to learn to use a computer. This book may be used as a textbook for educational or corporate trainers, teachers, educators, library media specialists, and individuals. Screen captures, illustrations, step-by-step directions, resources, design principles, tips throughout, and an index make this book very user-friendly. Basic building blocks of digital stories, covered in the opening chapter, are also very useful as students learn to create or find digital videos, digital sounds, and digital images.

The "Resources" section of the Flash chapter includes images that can be scanned and prepared for use in developing the digital story. The Photoshop Elements tutorial in Appendix B should assist in the preparation of these images for the Flash story.

Chapter 1

Introducing "Digital Storytelling"

If you think that Disney is the only mega corporation interested in stories, think again. Did you know that the world's largest computer company and the world's leading technology university have research groups devoted to storytelling? That's right. IBM's and MIT's media labs are learning how stories are quite possibly the core of our intelligence. Research groups at these institutions are analyzing storytelling research from a number of disciplines, including sociolinguistics, anthropology, sociology, management sciences, and psychology. In 1990, two researchers wrote about a possible connection between storytelling and how our brain works. Roger Schank, one of the world's leading researchers in artificial intelligence and learning theory, wrote *Tell Me a Story*, which proposed that the core of intelligence is accessing specific concrete narrative stories (Schank, Chapters 1, 2, and 7). In *Acts of Meaning*, internationally renowned psychologist Jerome Bruner credits Jean Mandler's finding that "what does not get structured narratively suffers loss in memory" (Bruner p.56). He also stated that without narrative storytelling skills "we could never endure the conflicts and contradictions that social life generates" (Bruner p.97). Bruner basically posed that our brains are wired in narrative stories.

Interestingly, at the same time that these researchers were highlighting the importance of storytelling, the late creative visionary Dana Atchley III was beginning the digital storytelling movement. In the 1990s, he was well known for his digital storytelling in his autobiographical performances titled "Next Exit." In 1994, he also collaborated with Joe Lambert and Nina Mullen to found the San Francisco Digital Media Center. In 1995, he and his wife Denise founded the *Digital Storytelling Conference & Festival* that ran annually until his untimely death in 2000.

What Is Digital Storytelling?

For thousands of years the best storytellers told stories around the campfire. With the fire dancing and smoke rising, at early dusk or late in the night, great storytellers captivated audiences with all kinds of tales. Anyone who has been captivated by an expert at this craft will not soon forget it. Over the last several decades, expert storytellers found that they could reach new audiences with newer technologies. For years, those families who could afford it would gather around the high tech campfire called a radio and would listen to stories told over the airwaves. More recently, the television has replaced other forms of media and has become the number one storyteller in our lives. The average American spends hours a day glued to this modern raconteur. In 2002, all commercial television stations in America were regulated to begin transmitting a digital signal, instead of the older analog signal. In a sense, the stories seen on television may now be considered digital stories. The exciting thing about this transition is that the digital storytelling tools of the television industry are now becoming available to the masses by way of the computer. Inexpensive digital tools and new software have literally put the power of a Hollywood director into the hands of the average person. Now, literally anyone with an interest has the ability to create digital stories for use around the digital campfires.

More technically, digital refers to information that is expressed as digits like 1 or 0 (binary) or as #FB012C (hexadecimal), which are both numerical systems that computers can understand. Basically, digital storytelling is telling a story created in a digital format, most often by using a computer. By integrating a variety of digital media together, which may include audio, video, pictures, and images, the storytellers of tomorrow are creating digital stories that can be watched on televisions, computers, personal digital assistants (PDAs), or game stations. As digital information, these stories can be easily stored, archived, transferred, or manipulated.

Who's Telling Digital Stories and Why?

Everyone has a story to tell. So what's your electronic story? Perhaps that question might be easier to answer after looking at who's telling digital stories. One grandparent digitally archived her family's history to pass on to her grandchildren. A university secretary digitized decades of memorable photographs, narrated stories that went with those photographs, and added her parents' favorite song when she created a video celebrating their 50th wedding anniversary. A Boy Scout and his father cataloged the journey to becoming an Eagle Scout. More generally, many diverse groups of people are benefiting from telling digital stories, including corporations, educators, survivors, and activists. Anyone can tell digital stories.

Corporations are discovering how to use storytelling to sell products, build communities, and create what their knowledge organization divisions refer to as "social capital." In part, this refers to the management, maintenance, and development of "real life" product related stories that carry powerful emotional associations that may be leveraged to create emotional attachments toward companies. The Coca-Cola Company was one of the first corporations to see how digital storytelling could help it collect social capital. It collected product related digital stories from around the world at the 1996 Olympics in

Atlanta. The best of these stories have been integrated into kiosk-style presentations at the Coca-Cola museum in Atlanta. In reality, this museum is a collection of very positive, product related stories. IBM and Xerox are two other corporations with research labs studying how storytelling will be a critical component of corporate success.

For education, literally thousands of students and teachers are telling digital stories. From preschool through graduate school, students are integrating these stories into portfolios and projects. Scholars and library media specialists are developing captivating stories for use in multimedia-enhanced presentations. Experts within the educational arena realize that digital stories are more engaging, interesting, and memorable for students. They may be more accurate also. There are certain subjects, such as history, geography, and science, which are best not left to the imagination.

Examples of "survivors" that are getting very good results from digital stories include veterans of foreign wars, former cancer patients, and victims of rape and domestic violence. They are finding that they can create powerful and emotional narratives that teach and tell their stories.

Activists are also utilizing digital stories to help support and give voice to social and environmental campaigns. For example, ecologist Adam Werbach, former Sierra Club president, launched Act Now Productions to develop digital environmental stories that weren't being told anywhere else.

Introducing eStories to Students

Tech savvy teachers and library media specialists are certainly capable of integrating digital storytelling into schools. In fact, these types of projects easily adapt themselves to collaboration between library media specialists and classroom teachers. The library media specialist may be the ideal partner in this type of project because:

1. some of the projects include a research component,
2. library media specialists are often good sources of technical support,
3. the library media center is often an appropriate place for project development and student presentations,
4. collaboration is currently being stressed in education with such practices as vertical and grade level teaming being implemented,
5. information literacy crosses all curriculum areas, and
6. the library media specialist can potentially offer a great service to classroom teachers with books, Web sites, and other materials related to these projects.

Introducing students to digital storytelling can be done using materials gleaned from the first chapter of this book or from the *Digital Storytelling Cookbook and Travelling Companion* (listed in the "Resources" section for the Premiere chapter). Perhaps a better way is to personally develop a digital story for the purpose of presenting it to the students. When developing a digital story, people often discover that some of the best stories are built around simplistic ideas. This is particularly important when first starting. Focus on developing a very short story, and then tell it well. After students develop confidence in the tools, and in the methods and techniques of digital storytelling, it is only natural that their stories will become more elaborate and more complicated. But in the beginning, keep it simple to survive. All the digital stories developed in this book are relatively short and are fairly easy to tell with images and sometimes sound.

What is Needed to Create Digital Stories

For the most part, developing digital stories requires the use of hardware and software. On the hardware side, a multimedia-enabled computer, complete with speakers and a microphone, is recommended. A scanner, a digital camera, and a digital video camera are tools of the trade that are nice to have but are not always necessary. On the software side, any of the programs covered in this book will suffice, depending on exactly what is being created. It is important to note that many of these software programs presume that the images, sounds, and movie clips to be used have already been prepared in a separate program. That means users may first need to invest in a sound-editing, an image-editing, or a digital video-editing program in addition to the basic storytelling software. In this book, the sound elements that are created utilize a basic application that comes standard on all Windows Operating Systems. For image editing, our recommendation is to use an inexpensive program called Photoshop Elements. A basic tutorial for this program is featured in Appendix B. For digital video editing, two of the programs covered in this book, Studio and Premiere, are appropriate.

Additionally, the Internet can provide truckloads of sounds, images, and movie clips, all just a click away. Before hauling loads of this material into your project, it is good to be familiar with federal copyright law and to understand the fair-use guidelines and a few basic intellectual property rights. These will be covered at the end of this chapter.

Getting Started with Storyboards

When beginning to work on a story, you can begin with a storyboard, or an outline, of the way the digital story is supposed to look when finished. Completing a storyboard not only assists in the organization of a project but also in its efficiency, saving a great deal of time in the long run. A good storyboard helps keep track of the different types of media to be used and includes a timeline of when to use that media. In fact, for best results, it is recommended that you not even turn on the computer until this basic plan is developed. Storyboards can be created with anything from scratch paper and a pen to special software programs designed for the task.

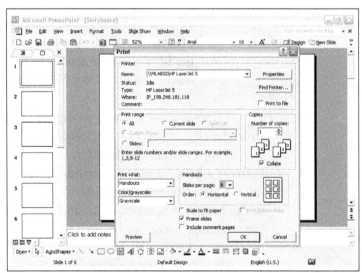

Figure 1.1: Creating a storyboard in PowerPoint

For many of the examples in the book, Microsoft PowerPoint was used to create a storyboard template consisting of six (or nine) blank slides. To do this, first create a new slide show and add six (or nine) blank slides to the show by clicking on the **New Slide** button. Then print these blank slides in the *Handouts* view, by selecting **File > Print**. Click on the down arrow and select *Handouts* in the bottom-left corner of the *Print* window, under the heading *Print what*. To the right of *Slides per page*, select the number of blank slides needed for your storyboard and then press **OK**. The basic storyboard and one other more detailed storyboard can be found in Appendix A. These can be copied or scanned and printed and used to create a story.

Storytelling Software

What software is needed to tell digital stories? The classic favorite, taught in the past at the *Digital Storytelling Festival's Boot Camp*, has been Adobe Premiere, a digital video-editing program. Premiere allows users to integrate a variety of media into a final production. For example, still images, graphics, narration, sound effects, and music can be combined in any number of ways, with or without digital video, to create a final video production. Video created in Premiere may be viewed in the leading Web and video formats, including VCR, DVD, and MPEG-2. This high-end program is one of the more complex programs covered in this book.

On the other end of the spectrum, preschoolers and early elementary education students are creating their stories by using programs like Kid Pix and Broderbund's PrintShop. In fact, even before the digital storytelling movement got started, former elementary school librarian Dave Titus <http://www.storyteller-wordsmith.com> encouraged students to develop PrintShop mini-stories by writing short one, two, or three page stories and adding a picture. The final story could be viewed on screen or could be printed out, folded, and presented to parents in the form of a card. With a little help from Dave Titus, the story in Figure 1.2 is a good example of those created by students when he visited the school library in 1985.

The software programs covered in this book progress from simple to complex with each new chapter. The first program, Kid Pix, is clearly the easiest and can be used with preschoolers. As a drawing program, with a good number of flags and maps available, this program can be used at any elementary school level and contains numerous ideas, spanning most of the classroom disciplines, for classroom application. Students can easily convert their art into slides that can be used in a presentation. Studio is an award winning video-editing program that is relatively simple. This program features an easy-to-use interface that allows the user to drag and drop captured video footage onto a timeline, making it easy for upper elementary students to learn the program. Additionally, students can add 3D transitions, background music, and many

Figure 1.2: PrintShop Story by Dirk, Second Grade, Mrs. Bowling's class

other special effects to create impressive CDs, DVDs, or VCR tapes. PowerPoint, a presentation program, is next and is relatively easy to learn. Third graders at some schools are required to demonstrate final projects in PowerPoint. PowerPoint is robust enough that it could be used throughout the schooling experience. Premiere is a high-end digital video-editing program. Documentary-style programs produced for broadcast television could be created with this program. Middle school and high school students are creating school-based news programs as well as basic digital stories, in which still photographs are made to look as if they were video clips, with Premiere. Flash is the final program we use to create a digital story. It is arguably the most complex program covered in this book. This Web-authoring program is most often used to create dynamic Web sites. It is also used to create cartoon-based digital stories for online audiences.

Digital Media

Digital Images
Generally, the core of a digital story is built around pictures and clip art. A student once remarked that it took him over three hours of surfing online to find the image he was looking for. He was doing a project on Amelia Earhart and was searching for an animated .gif of a biplane flying over water. The image certainly helped put his project on par with professionally designed projects. It should be noted that a library media specialist, teaching keyword searching, could certainly have saved this student some time.

Image File Types
There are a number of image file types, including .bmp, .gif, .jpg, .png, and .tif. Definitions for each of these image types can be found in the glossary at the end of this chapter. When working with images, the file type is sometimes not listed as part of the name. To find out what type of file the image is, *right* click on the file and select **Properties** from the drop-down menu.

Software for Images
Appendix B features a tutorial covering an excellent image-editing software program called Adobe Photoshop Elements. If that is not available, another excellent image editing resource that is worth checking out is online at <http://myimager.com>. This online image-editing software was listed as one of the 50 most useful sites on the Internet by Yahoo! in 2002. Crop, retouch, and brighten images all online. No special software is needed. Also add text, rotate, flip, or convert images to black and white. One limitation is that .jpg and .gif files cannot exceed 200KB.

Downloading Images
After locating a desired image on the Internet, downloading it to the computer or disk is easy. *Right* click on the image and a menu will drop down. (Note: Certain types of images cannot be saved in this manner, and the following options will not appear.) Select **Download image to Disk** or **Save Picture As**. A *Save* or *Save Picture* dialog box will open. Choose a location to save the image. It is often best to rename the image at

this time, while leaving the period and last three letters of the image as part of the name. For example, if the image is currently named "0112039lix.jpg," rename it "redball.jpg" in order to identify what it is when it is needed later. In some of the newer browsers, the name and file type are separate. In the browser pictured, change the file

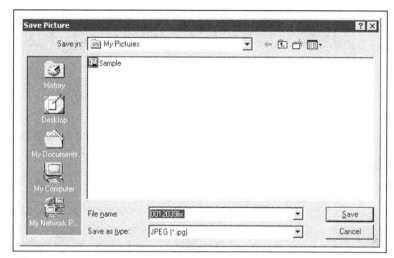

Figure 1.3: Image Save As

name to "redball" and leave the **Save as type** as a JPEG (*.jpg). Note that the arrow to the right of the text box can be changed to Bitmap (*.bmp) if desired. For a listing of some excellent online image resources, see the "Resources" section in the final chapter.

Digital Sounds

There are a large number of sound file types, but for our purposes, the most useful are MP3 and .wav files (see glossary for definitions). To find sound clips online, a great place to begin is Altavista's <http://www.altavista.com> search engine (click on the **Audio** tab at the top of the *Search* window).

For audio software, Sound Forge is an excellent program for editing sound; however, none of the stories in this book require anything more than the Sound Recorder that comes standard with Windows Operating Systems. Simply go to **Programs > Accessories > Entertainment > Sound Recorder** to open this handy little utility that allows users to save narrations, sounds, and music to a .wav file.

Digital Movie Clips

Although there are a number of movie file types, .avi or .mov file types (see glossary) are most useful for our purposes. To find movie clips online, a great place to begin is Altavista's <http://www.altavista.com> search engine (click on the **Video** tab at the top of the *Search* window). Over half a million media clips are indexed here. To find the movie clip, from the movie *Jerry McGuire*, where Tom Cruise says, "Help me, Help You," type quotes around the exact phrase and then type the kind of file. For example: "Help me, Help you" mov. This will prompt a search for a .mov (QuickTime) file with that phrase. For additional options, select the **Advanced Search** option.

To download movie clips or sounds, click on the hyperlink to the clip. A *File Download* dialog box should open. Select the **Save this file to disk** option and choose **OK**. Choose the location where you want to save the movie or sound clip.

Intellectual Property Rights

Before getting too excited about implementing some of the ideas found in this book, make sure to obtain the proper permissions necessary for creating these types of stories. An educator might expend a lot of time and energy developing the "Student of the Week" video projects for the purpose of creating a digital class yearbook and Web site. However, some parents may be adamantly opposed to having their children pictured digitally for any reason. Child abduction, custody battles, stalking, and identity theft are just a few of the issues that parents wrestle with today. Educators would do well to think through these issues and to design their projects with these issues in mind. Parental permission should be obtained before these types of projects begin. A simple parental agreement form can be sent home with students outlining the project before starting.

Four Simple Fair-Use Guidelines for Multimedia Projects

One of the questions most frequently asked by students when they are designing digital stories is, "Can I use a song from a CD I purchased?" Music can certainly spice up a digital story. Adding music clips from Brittany Spears or Garth Brooks can give any project the polish and energy of a professional creation. Instead of going through the process of getting permission from the copyright owners, it may be easier to follow a few simple guidelines before inserting any media into a project.

1. Fair-Use Limit
Fair-use guidelines clearly limit the amount of copyrighted materials students, scholars, and educators may use. Here are the two guidelines that are often abused:

- **Music** — 10% or 30 seconds of a song (whichever is less), and
- **Video** — 10% or three minutes (whichever is less).

"Whichever is less" is important. If a song lasts three minutes (180 seconds), only 18 seconds can be used because in this case 10% of the song "is less" than 30 seconds. Savvy students and educators generate lists of songs that are at least five minutes long in order to use the maximum length of 30 seconds. Sound software, like Sonic Foundry, allows users to find a section at the beginning and end of a clip that will loop nicely. Segments can be looped continuously and played as background music.

2. Legitimate Copy
Another factor to remember when using media clips is to use a legitimate, "lawfully acquired" copy of the song or video. Using an MP3 clip found online does not constitute legal use.

3. Warning Label
At the beginning of the project, a warning label should be prominently placed that states something to the effect that "the audio and video clips in this presentation are used

under fair-use guidelines and are restricted from further use." There is no specific wording that belongs in this label.

4. Specific Credit
Credit should be given in a Bibliography or Mediography at the end of the project. Be sure to include the copyright symbol (©), the year the media was first published, and the name of the copyright owner.

Public Domain

Media found in the public domain is generally free to use and does not require following the fair-use guidelines or obtaining copyright permission. Material may be in the public domain because the copyright has expired. Examples of this would apply to compositions published in the United States before 1923, like those of Tchaikovsky and Beethoven. Although not as common as it once was, this is the reason that cartoons often use classical music in their sound tracks. Remember, though, if you want to use the 1812 Overture in your production, make sure to use your own orchestra to play it. Purchasing the CD of the Boston Philharmonic playing the 1812 Overture would not be included in the public domain. This is because the CD carries the Boston Philharmonic's interpretation of the Overture. Once its interpretation is 75 years old, its version of the 1812 Overture will fall into the realm of public domain.

Another source of material found in the public domain is anything created by U.S. government employees within the course of their duties. Government Internet sites, designated by .gov or .mil, are often sources of these copyright-free materials for U.S. citizens. Materials created at these sites are generated, at least in part, by taxes paid by U.S. citizens. Care should be taken, as not everything at these sites is free. Links to commercial Web sites and artist's images on postage stamps are two examples from government sites that would not fall in the public domain.

Resources

Short Chronology of the Digital Storytelling Movement

- <http://www.nextexit.com> Early 1990s — Dana Atchley III is widely recognized as having coined the term "digital storytelling." He was well known for theatrical presentations of his digital autobiography titled "Next Exit."
- <http://www.storycenter.org> 1994 — Joe Lambert, Nina Mullen, and Dana Atchley founded the San Francisco Digital Media Center.
- <http://www.dstory.com> 1995 — Denise Atchley, along with husband Dana, founded the *Digital Storytelling Conference & Festival*. This annual festival ran between 1995 and 1999. With Dana's death in 2000, the festival has been indefinitely canceled.

Who's Telling Digital Stories?

- \<http://europe.cnn.com/TECH/9703/11/digital.story\> CNN—Oral history goes high tech: Stories for posterity told with multimedia. March 1, 1997, by Greg Lefevre.

Corporations

- \<http://www.research.ibm.com/knowsoc\> IBM lists several benefits when businesses use stories. Stories helped build social capital and community. This contextualized knowledge increases trusted accountability, which leads to lower hiring and training costs and better teamwork efficiency. Another benefit is that stories are memorable and motivating which means that people will remember them overtime.
- \<http://www.research.ibm.com/knowsoc/presentation/indexp42.htm\> and \<http://www2.parc.com/ops/members/brown/storytelling\> Xerox—Storytelling: Passport to Success in the 21st Century.

Educators

- \<http://www.scott.k12.ky.us/technology/digitalstorytelling/ds.html\> Scott County Digital Storytelling Web site.
- \<http://www.media.mit.edu/groups/gn\> The Gesture and Narrative Language research group at the MIT Media Lab is conducting nearly two-dozen research projects that combine technology and storytelling.

Survivors

- \<http://www.silencespeaks.org/resources.html\> Links provided include: for abuse survivors, the healing room, the survivor advocates page, the Survivors' Art Foundation, the Survivors' Page, and the Widows of War Living Memorial.

Activists

- \<http://www.actnowproductions.com\> Adam Werbach, former Sierra Club president, is developing digital environmental stories.
- \<http://www.silencespeaks.org/resources.html\> Link and description provided here for the Video Activist Network.

Glossary

avi: Audio/Video (pronounced "A-V-I")—This Microsoft standard movie file works well on PCs.

bmp: Graphic image—Bitmaps are a standard Microsoft Windows graphic format.

jpg: Graphic image (pronounced J-Peg)—Great for pictures and photographs (millions of colors).

gif: Graphic image (the preferred pronunciation is with a hard g like "go")—Great for cartoons and icons (limited to only 256 colors).

mov: Audio/Video (pronounced "M-O-V")—This is a standard format used on the Macintosh operating system, but it requires a QuickTime Player for playing on PCs.

MP3: Sound file (pronounced "M-P-3")—This very popular sound file format compresses sounds for compact storage but requires an MP3 player.

png: Graphic image (pronounced "ping")—Pings can be either indexed as 256-color images or can have 16.7 million true colors.

tiff: Graphic image—Save scanned images as TIFFs unless scanning directly into Photoshop, in which case save as a .psd (Photoshop file). After edits, you can always convert the image to .gif or .jpg.

wav: Sound file (pronounced "wave")—This very common sound file format is the standard sound for Windows machines, yet it works very well on Macs.

Chapter 2

Goal Setting with Kid Pix Delux 3

What I Want to Be When I Grow Up

Introduction

Kid Pix Delux 3 is an interactive paint and presentation software program for preschool through elementary levels. It is an affordable, a user-friendly, and an aesthetically pleasing program, with many features for home and school use.

In this chapter students will create a digital story depicting what they want to be when they are grown. After following the example provided, students and teachers should be familiar with many of the software's features, thus reaching the level of comfort necessary to create and present their own digital stories.

Materials Needed

- Kid Pix Delux 3
- Digital Pictures (see relevant sections of Chapter 1 and Appendix B)
  - Child
  - Forest fire (can be retrieved from an Internet search)

A Look at the Completed Project

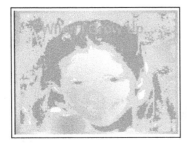

Figure 2.1: Slide 1

Figure 2.2: Slide 2

Figure 2.3: Slide 3

Figure 2.4: Slide 4

Figure 2.5: Slide 5

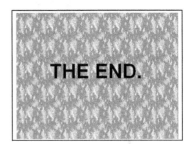

Figure 2.6: Slide 6

Kid Pix Delux 3 © 2000 Riverdeep Interactive Learning Limited. All rights reserved. Used with permission

Getting Started with a Storyboard

Figure 2.7: Kid Pix Storyboard

Building the Project

1. Save a picture of a child and a forest fire in a file titled *Student Photos* on the Desktop. Save each image as a .jpg.
2. Open the Kid Pix Delux 3 program. Turn up the computer's speaker volume to hear the program's sounds. To bypass the music at the beginning, click on the screen to bring up the *Sign In* window.
3. Enter your name in the box provided and press **GO**. The *Paint Zone* screen will appear.

Figure 2.8: Sign In Window

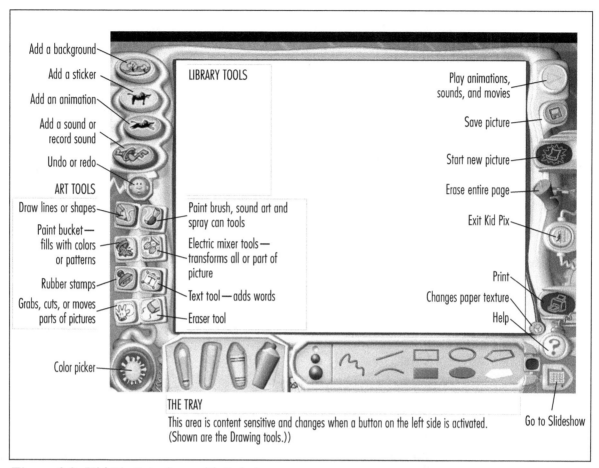

Add a background
Add a sticker
Add an animation
Add a sound or record sound
Undo or redo

ART TOOLS

LIBRARY TOOLS

Draw lines or shapes
Paint bucket— fills with colors or patterns
Rubber stamps
Grabs, cuts, or moves parts of pictures

Paint brush, sound art and spray can tools
Electric mixer tools— transforms all or part of picture
Text tool—adds words
Eraser tool

Color picker

Play animations, sounds, and movies
Save picture
Start new picture
Erase entire page
Exit Kid Pix
Print
Changes paper texture
Help

THE TRAY
This area is content sensitive and changes when a button on the left side is activated. (Shown are the Drawing tools.))

Go to Slideshow

Figure 2.9: Kid Pix Interface with Labels

The large white space in the middle of the *Paint Zone* represents a blank canvas or the *Drawing Area*. The buttons surrounding the *Drawing Area* are tools for creating a picture.

Getting Help

1. The **Help** button (bottom right of screen) explains the function of the tools, buttons, and interface. Click on the **Help** button; then press on a part of the screen for a brief explanation of its function; then press **OK**.

   Click on the **Background** button to bring up the explanatory *Help* window (Figure 2.12).

Figure 2.10: Help Button

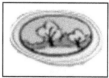

Figure 2.11: Background Button

Figure 2.12: Help Window

2. Another way to obtain help is to consult the program's User Guide. Access
the *Menu Bar* by placing the mouse at
the top of the screen. When a
Triangle button appears, press and hold down the mouse button.
The *Menu Bar* will appear.

Figure 2.13:
Triangle Button

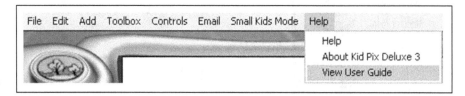

Figure 2.14: Help > View User Guide

3. Select **Help**; then drag the mouse down until **View User Guide** is highlighted and click on it. The User Guide will open with Acrobat Reader.
View or print the directions for using the program.

Erasing Mistakes

There are several ways to erase a mistake.

1. The **Undo Guy** button is located on
the left side of the screen. By clicking
on him, the last action completed will
automatically be erased. (Note: There
is only one level of undo in this program.)

Figure 2.15: Undo
Guy Button

2. If the **Undo Guy** won't erase what
you want from the *Drawing Area*,
select the **Eraser** button located in the
bottom left of the screen.

Figure 2.16: Eraser Button

Figure 2.17: Eraser Tray

After selecting the **Eraser** button, the *Eraser Tray* will appear.
For erasing small areas, choose the small pencil eraser. For bigger areas,
choose the larger eraser. The size of
the eraser may also be changed by
selecting one of the three different-
sized circles (representing small,
medium, and large) within the tray.

Figure 2.18: Eraser Sizes

3. Press **Ctrl + Z** to undo the last command or press **Ctrl + Y** to redo it.
4. To start over completely, select the **New Picture** button on the right side of the screen.
5. For a more entertaining way of erasing the picture, start over with a bang by clicking on the **Firecracker** button located on the right side of the screen.

Figure 2.19: New Picture Button

Figure 2.20: Firecracker Button

Adding Graphics

1. Since this digital story will feature what students want to be when they grow up, begin by adding a photo of a child. Access the *Menu Bar*; then select **Add > Add Graphic**.
2. When the *Add Graphic* dialog box appears, select the correct image format and navigate to the *Student Photos* file on the Desktop. Select the picture and press **Open** or **OK**. After locating the photo previously saved, select **Center at Original Size** and press **OK**. The photo will appear in the *Drawing Area*.

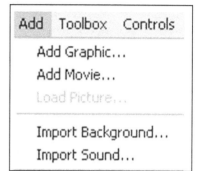

Figure 2.21: Add > Add Graphic

Figure 2.22: Student Picture in the Drawing Area

3. To resize the picture, click on any of the **Resize** buttons (located in the corners of the graphic) and drag until the picture is the preferred size.

 Figure 2.23: Resize Button

4. Save the picture. While continuing to work in Kid Pix, remember to periodically save the picture by clicking on the **Save** button on the right side of the screen or by pressing **Ctrl + S** on the keyboard.

 Figure 2.24: Save Button

Mixing it Up

1. To add interest to the plain-looking photo, select the **Electric Mixer** button. The *Mixers Tray* will appear.

 Figure 2.25: Electric Mixer Button

Figure 2.26: Mixers Tray

To alter the look of the entire photo, click on the large **Mega Mixer** tool.

2. Notice the up and down arrows located on the far right side of the *Mixers Tray*.

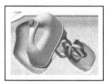 **Figure 2.27:** Mega Mixer Tool

3. Click on the down arrow to view all of the mixing options. When the digital number between the two arrows reads "02," stop and select the fourth square from the left.

Click on the picture in the *Drawing Area* to alter the picture.

 Figure 2.28: Up and Down Arrows

4. After finishing this first picture, save it and create a new one by selecting the **New Picture** button on the right side of the screen.

 Figure 2.29: Mixer Choice

 **Figure 2.19:** New Picture Button

Adding a Sticker (An Object)

Creating the Second Picture

1. Click on the **Sticker** button.
   The *Sticker Tray* will appear.
2. In the *Sticker Tray*, select the *Objects* category
   and choose the fire extinguisher using the up
   and down arrows on the right side of the
   Sticker Tray. With the extinguisher selected,
   drag the sticker to the *Drawing Area* and resize
   the image using the resize buttons located in
   the upper-left and bottom-right corners of the
   frame surrounding the sticker.
3. Flatten the sticker so that it becomes part of
   the background in order to place images over
   the fire extinguisher by selecting **Toolbox >
   Flatten Stickers and Animations**. (Note:
   Flattening images will eliminate any animation
   and sound effects.)

Figure 2.2: Slide 2—
Fire Extinguisher

Figure 2.30:
Sticker Button

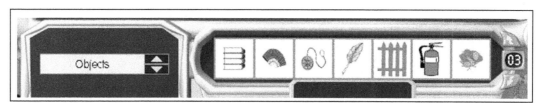

Figure 2.31: Sticker Tray

Adding Text

1. To add text to a picture, click on the **Text**
   button on the left side of the screen.
   The *Text Tray* will appear.

Figure 2.32: Text
Button

Figure 2.33: Text Tray

2. Click on the middle of the picture and type, "I want to be a"

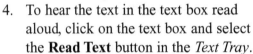

Figure 2.34: Text Box

3. To edit the appearance of the text, locate the **Formatting Options** on the left side of the *Text Tray*. Press and hold down on the *Font* window to view the list of fonts. Click on the black arrow at the top and bottom to reveal the entire list and begin scrolling to find the **Arial** font. Click on the **Bold** option to make the text stand out in the picture, and click on the **Center** option to center the text.

Figure 2.35: Bold Button

Figure 2.36: Center Button

4. To hear the text in the text box read aloud, click on the text box and select the **Read Text** button in the *Text Tray*.

    Push the **Play** button to hear the text being read.

    Change the voice by clicking on the up or down arrows next to the voice name in the *Text Tray*.

Figure 2.37:
Read Text Button

Figure 2.38: Play Button

Moving and Deleting

1. To move the text to a new position, click on the **Grab** button on the left side of the screen.

    The *Grab Tray* should appear.

Figure 2.39: Grab Button

Figure 2.40: Grab Tray

2. Select the **Hand**; then click on the text box. A frame will appear around it. To move the text, press on the top of the frame surrounding the text and drag it to its new position.

3. Tip: To delete the text box, click on it and press the **Delete** key on the keyboard.

Adding Animated Graphics

1. In this picture, the word "firefighter" will be animated. Click on the **Animation** button to bring up the *Animation Tray*.

Figure 2.41:
Animation Button

Figure 2.42: Animation Tray

2. Find and choose the *Alphabet* folder. Locate and select the letter "f" using the up and down arrows on the right side of the *Animation Tray*. Drag the letter to the picture and resize it using one of the **Resize** buttons located in upper-left and bottom-right corners of the frame surrounding the animation. Repeat this procedure for the rest of the letters needed to write the word "firefighter."

3. To view the animation, press the **Play** button and watch the letters come alive.

Paint Options

1. Select the **Painting Tools** button on the left side of the screen to bring up the *Paint Tray*.

Figure 2.43:
Painting Tools Button

Figure 2.44: Painting Tools Tray

Figure 2.45:
Moving Paint

2. For this picture add flames. Select the **Spray Can** tool (third tool from the left) and choose the **Moving Paint** mode.

    Using the up and down arrows on the right side of the *Paint Tray*, arrow down until the digital number between the two arrows reads "02." Select the flames (the second square from the left).

3. Click anywhere in the *Drawing Area* to paint flames on the picture.

Figure 2.2: Slide 2—
Fire Extinguisher

Creating a Background

The next picture will feature a city with buildings on fire using a pre-made background.

1. Select the **New Picture** button on the right side of the screen; then click on the **Background** button to bring up the *Background Tray*.

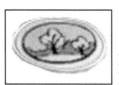

Figure 2.11: Background Button

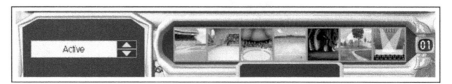

Figure 2.46: Background Tray

2. Select the folder titled *Color Me*. Arrow down to "02;" then click and drag the city scene (the second background from the left) into the *Drawing Area*.

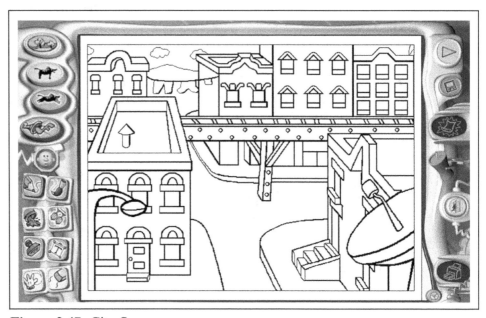

Figure 2.47: City Scene

Painting the Background

Figure 2.48:
Fill Bucket Button

1. To add color to the city scene, click on the **Fill Bucket** and fill in the selected areas of the picture with a color chosen in the *Color Picker*.

2. To access the *Color Picker*, click on the **Color Splotch** button in the bottom-left corner of the screen.

    In the example, a shade of gray was chosen from the *Color Picker*.

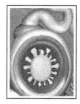

Figure 2.49:
Color Splotch

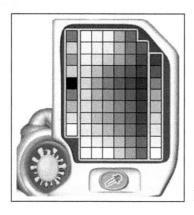

Figure 2.50: Color Picker

3. Use the **Solid Fill Bucket** to fill the city streets and sidewalks with color. The **Pattern Fill Bucket** could also be used to fill the buildings, for example, with a brick pattern.

Figure 2.51:
Solid Fill Bucket

Figure 2.52:
Pattern Fill Bucket

Adding Rubber Stamps

After coloring in the city, add fire to the buildings.

Figure 2.53:
Rubber Stamp Button

1. Click on the **Rubber Stamp** button on the left side of the screen to access the *Rubber Stamp Tray*.

Figure 2.54: Rubber Stamp Tray

2. To add flames to the picture, choose the *Adventure* folder; then select the **Flames** stamp (the first stamp from the left) and click on one of the building's windows in the *Drawing Area*.

Figure 2.55: Flames Stamp

Add additional objects to the city by using the **Stamp** button. Stamps of a fire truck and a fire hydrant can be found in the *City* folder.

3. Insert the text "I want to save people" near the middle of the slide.

Adding Music, Narration, and Sounds

Figure 2.56: Sound Button

1. Click on the **Sound** button on the left side of the screen to access the *Sound Tray*.

Figure 2.57: Sound Tray

2. Choose the folder titled *Everyday* and arrow down to the second set of available sounds. Select **Traffic** sound on the far right of the *Sound Tray* and drag it into the *Drawing Area*. Press the **Play** button to listen to the sound at any time.

Importing a Background

1. For the background of the next picture, use an image of a forest fire saved previously in the *Student Photos* folder on the Desktop. To import a background image, access the *Menu Bar*; then select **Add > Import Background**.
2. After locating the previously saved image file, press **OK**. The photo should appear covering the entire space of the *Drawing Area*.
3. Add the text "forests from burning ..." at the bottom of the picture; then save and name the picture.

Figure 2.58: Forest Fire

4. The fifth slide uses the **Color Me** background. Select the **Street** scene and color the image. Add the text "... and even cats stuck in trees!" and stamp a cat in the tree (look in the category *Animal*). Save and name the picture.

5. The last slide contains a patterned fill background of fires. Select the **Paint Bucket** button and select the **Pattern Bucket** from the *Paint Tray*. Select the fire pattern and add the text "The End." Save and name the picture.

Figure 2.5: Slide 5—
Street Scene

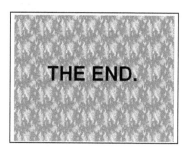

Figure 2.6: Slide 6—
The End

Printing

1. To print the picture at any time, simply click the **Print** button located at the bottom right of the screen.

2. In the *Print This Picture* dialog box, choose whether to print the picture in Full Page or Poster format. Make sure the printer is powered on and press **OK**.

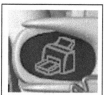

Figure 2.59:
Print Button

Creating a Slide Show

Creating slide shows with pictures created in Kid Pix gives students the opportunity to present their stories to others.

Figure 2.60:
Slide Show Button

1. To create a slide show, click the **Slide Show** button in the bottom-right corner of the *Paint Zone* screen.

   The *Slide Show* screen will appear.

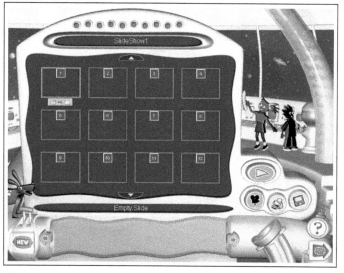

Figure 2.61: Slide Show Screen

2. Click on the icon shaped like a folder to load a picture into the frame.

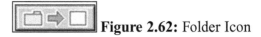

Figure 2.62: Folder Icon

   In the *Load Picture* dialog box, select the desired picture and press **Open**.

3. Click on the **Slide Show Effect** button to add transitions and sounds to the slide.

Figure 2.63: Slide Show Effect Button

   Red arrows will appear before each frame.

4. Click on the red arrow before the slide to bring up the *Select Transition and Sound* dialog box. Select a transition and sound for the slide and press the **Preview** button to observe the added effects. When satisfied press **OK**.

Figure 2.64: Select Transition and Sound Window

Adaptations and Extensions

Other Ideas to Explore

- **Adding Movies.** To add a QuickTime movie to your digital story, access the *Menu Bar* and click **Add > Add Movie**. Add an original QuickTime movie or insert any one of the pre-made movies included with Kid Pix. Locate the movie file to be added to the picture and click **Open** (pre-made QuickTime movies are located on the Kid Pix Delux 3 CD-ROM in the folder named *QT Movies*). At this point, the movie can be placed anywhere on the picture by clicking on the movie itself and dragging it to the appropriate location. To play the movie, press the **Play** button in the top-right corner of the screen. Experiment with different ways to display the movie within your picture. For example, make the movie appear as if it is playing on a television or movie screen. This can be achieved by adding a television graphic to the picture, or by locating one already included in the Kid Pix Delux 3 program, and then positioning and resizing the movie so it appears to be part of the television or movie screen graphic.

- **Idea Machine.** The *Idea Machine* is a good resource when creativity needs a little jump-start. It contains numerous pictures to choose from, draw on, color in, and customize in their entirety. To access the *Idea Machine*, select **Toolbox** in the *Menu Bar* and click on a picture. Press **Open** and, using your imagination, begin making someone else's idea your own.

- **Sound Art.** What would a sound look like if it could be drawn? To find out, try using *Sound Art*, one of the most innovative and intriguing features of Kid Pix. *Sound Art* creates art from any sound. To try this feature, click on the **Painting Tools** button to open the *Paint Tray*. Select *Sound Art* (represented by a microphone), which is located between the Paintbrush and the Spray Can in the *Paint Tray*. Then click on the **Hands-free** button to let your voice paint without the assistance of the computer's mouse. Using a microphone attached to your computer, say your name or sing your favorite song into the microphone and be amazed by the image that magically appears in the *Drawing Area*.

- **Spell-Checking.** To use this feature, access the *Menu Bar* and select **Toolbox > Check Spelling**. Kid Pix will proceed in spell-checking every text box in the picture. When finished spell-checking, press **Done**.

Curriculum Connections

It is easy to implement Kid Pix into any subject area. For "curriculum templates," click on the **Backgrounds** button and choose an appropriate template folder. Here are some possibilities:

- **Beginning of the School Activity.** Access the *All About Me* template for a great get-acquainted activity.
- **Scheduling and Organization.** Develop a class schedule, to do lists, and weekly and monthly calendars with templates found under *School Stuff*.
- **Math.** Check out the *Dots 2 Dot* template or develop a book of numbers under the *Numbers* templates. Create and study shapes using the drawing tools.

- **Health.** The *Foods I Eat* template has many possibilities.
- **Geography.** Create a report using the various maps and flags. Also check out the *Culture* templates.
- **Science.** Habitats and animals can be found under *Animal Projects*. Access the "My invention form" under *Idea Machine,* which is found in the **Toolbox** menu.
- **English/Writing/Journalism.** Check out *My Journal* and *Media Reports* to create student reviews for art, software, games, music, movies, books, and TV. Also check out the *Alphabet Book* templates.
- **Art.** Access the *Arts and Crafts* or *Masks* templates.
- **Music.** Work with *Sound Art* using the **Painting** tools.

Resources

- At this time, a free trial download of Kid Pix Delux 3 is not being offered. A preview of the program, however, may be accessed at <http://www.kidpix.com/par_kpd3.html>.
- For more information about this software and its uses in the classroom, visit the program's Web site located at <http://www.kidpix.com>. Painting online, submitting a "picture of the month," and viewing ideas to spark the imagination are just some of the options to be found on the Kid Pix Delux 3 Web site. In addition, links to individualized information for teachers, parents, and students are provided.

Glossary

Color Picker: A window or small color palette that includes the eye dropper and color splotch tools that allow for color selection.

Color Splotch: A button that opens the color palette for color selection.

Electric Mixer: Mixes up or alters your picture.

Mega Mixer: A selection of the Electric Mixer that mixes up the entire painting, whereas the Mini Mixer allows one to mix up parts of the painting.

Paint Zone: Paint Zone and Slide Show are the two main parts of Kid Pix. The Paint Zone is the painting view or portion of the program.

Sticker: A sticker floats above your picture like a balloon and cannot be erased with the eraser tool.

Transition Effect: Special effects between slides including cut, swipe, and dissolve.

Undo Guy: A button used to undo the last command or operation.

User Guide: Contains the help menu and step-by-step directions.

Chapter 3

Good "News" in Pinnacle Studio

You're the Student of the Week

Introduction

With an installed base of over two million users, the popular Pinnacle Studio is an excellent program for learning video production and editing skills. Pinnacle Systems is a leader in the video industry, recently winning its eighth Emmy, this time for technological advancement. Its newly released Studio 8 also won the prestigious Editor's Choice Award from *PC Magazine* (November 2002 issue). Months earlier, CNET.com reviewed over a dozen digital video-editing programs and rated Studio 7 as one of the very best programs. Surprisingly, it was also one of the most inexpensive programs at around $70.

The digital story for this chapter will honor a student selected as "Student of the Week." Ideas for extending this example in the classroom are far-reaching. Ideally, students in groups of two or three would be involved in all phases of their fellow student's video presentation, from interviewing the honoree to scanning photos of his or her best work to editing the video. The finished digital stories could then be uploaded to the school's Web site for viewing or could be combined into a single video that could be sold to parents at the end of the school year. In the interest of fairness, we would suggest that teachers applying this idea see that every student in class is awarded the title at least once during the school year. Studio 7 is both intuitive-to-use and easy on the pocketbook. Considering its affordability, there are an uncommonly high number of features in the software, making it a "must-have" for producing digital stories.

In this example, Autumn, an aspiring *and* inspiring young artist, was featured as this week's "Student of the Week." Using a digital video camera, Autumn was videotaped while she drew a picture. The camera kept taping when we interviewed her about her favorites (favorite color, movie, thing to do in school ...). Finally, digital photos illustrating some of her artwork were captured for inclusion in the video.

Materials Needed

- Multimedia-enabled computer with microphone and IEEE 1394/FireWire inputs
- Video Camera with IEEE 1394/FireWire computer enabled equipment or cables (Note: This project may be completed successfully without video, using only still images. For tips or suggestions see Chapter 1 and Appendix B for working with images in Photoshop Elements.)
- Pinnacle Studio 8 or 7 software
- Microphone
- Digital camera with equipment to move images onto the computer

A Look at the Completed Project

Here is what our "Student of the Week" video of Autumn looked like after editing it in Studio.

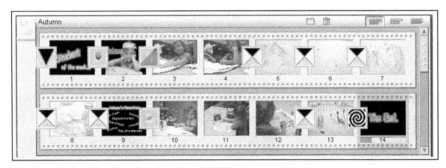

Figure 3.1: Student of the Week Video

Getting Started with a Storyboard

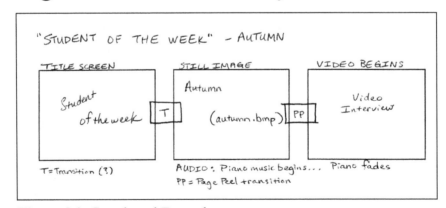

Figure 3.2: Storyboard Example

Building the Project

1. Create a folder on the Desktop named *Student of the Week*. Create a sub-folder inside the *Student of the Week* folder and name it *Pictures*. Insert any images in this movie. This could include scanned artwork or pictures taken with a digital camera and saved as a .jpg or .bmp.
2. Open Studio DV and begin creating the video as a new project. Select **File > New Project (Ctrl + N)** to begin.

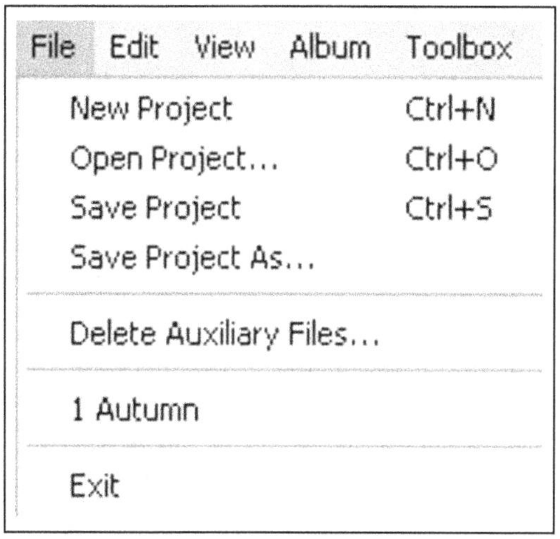

Figure 3.3: File > New Project

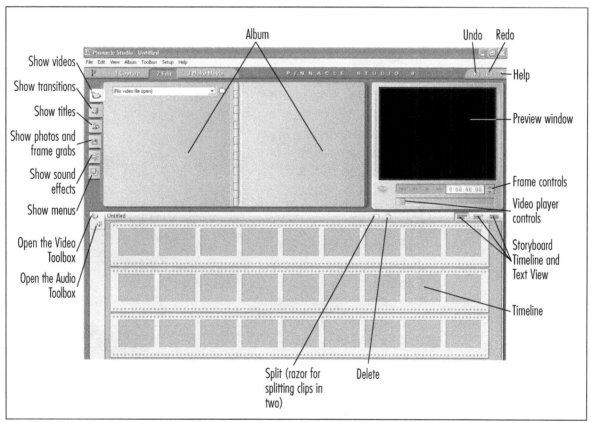

Figure 3.4: Studio Interface with Edit Tab and Storyboard View

3. To save the project, select **File > Save Project As** to bring up the *Save File* dialog. Name this project *Autumn* and save it to the *Student of the Week* folder by pressing **Save**. Periodically save the project by selecting **File > Save Project (Ctrl + S)**.

Capturing Video

1. After shooting four to eight minutes of the student interview, move the video onto the computer for editing. Most likely, this will require connecting the camera to the computer with an IEEE 1394/FireWire cable. (Note: After connecting our camera to the computer, the power had to be on with the camera set to VCR or VRT (videotape recorder) mode in order to complete the capturing video process.)

2. To begin capturing video from a video camera, select the **Capture** tab near the top left of the screen.

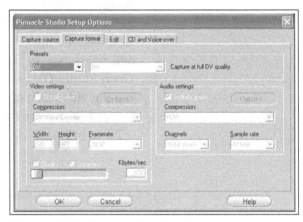

Figure 3.5: Capture Settings

3. Press the **Settings** button at the bottom right of the capture screen to bring up the *Setup Options* window. At this point, capture settings may be altered. For this "Student of the Week" video, the default settings are acceptable. Press **OK**.

4. Choose **DV full-quality capture**. [**7.0: Full-quality capture.**] Click on the **Start Capture** button in the bottom-right corner of the screen. As clips are captured, they will appear in the *Album*.

Figure 3.6: Capture Video

5. Enter a name for the capture in the *Capture Video* dialog box and press **Start Capture**.

6. Use the stop, fast-forward, play, and rewind buttons to find the particular place on the video to begin the capture. You may stop the capture at any time and then fast-forward to another scene to begin a new capture. Multiple captures can be combined in one movie. In this example, we are only using one capture.

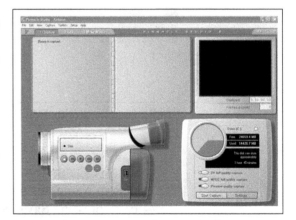

Figure 3.7: Capture Tab on Interface

Editing the Project

1. To begin editing the video, click on the **Edit** tab at the top of the screen.

Figure 3.8: Edit Tab

Take a moment to familiarize yourself with the layout of Studio 8 by clicking on each item on the *Menu Bar* and viewing the available options. For a better overview, go online and view the Flash tutorial listed in the "Resources" section at the end of this chapter.

2. On the right side of the screen, there are three buttons called **View Buttons**. Select each button and observe how the bottom half of the screen changes.

Figure 3.9: View Buttons

For this example, the *Storyboard* and *Timeline* views will be used. The *Storyboard* view is handy for organizing film clips (or scenes), images, and transitions, while the *Timeline* view is useful for inserting audio and sound files.

Figure 3.10: Icon for Storyboard View

- *Storyboard* View:

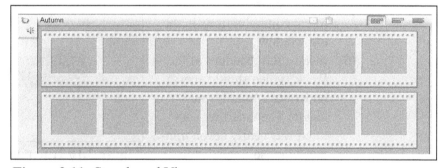

Figure 3.11: Storyboard View

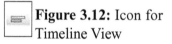

Figure 3.12: Icon for Timeline View

- *Timeline* View:

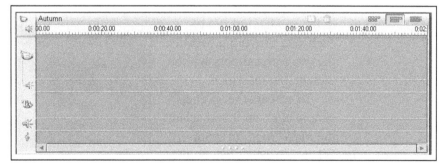

Figure 3.13: Timeline View

3. *Right* click on the captured image in the *Video Library* (top left) and select **Detect Scenes by Video Content** from the drop-down menu. This may help split the clip into more meaningful sections.

4. Select the **Storyboard** view. To move a scene, simply drag it onto the *Storyboard*. Drag and drop only those scenes that pertain to our project onto the *Storyboard*.

5. To edit a particular scene, open the *Video Toolbox* by clicking on the **Video Camera** button in the top-left corner of the *Storyboard*.

    A new window should appear. Notice the buttons on the left-hand side of the *Toolbox* window. Click on each one, observing the different editing options in the top window.

6. Ideally, the "Student of the Week" video should stay under three minutes in length. The video we captured was nearly seven minutes long, so it needed to be trimmed. To do this, select any clip in the *Storyboard* area and move the **Trim Calipers** horizontally while viewing the beginning and ending frames for that clip in the small windows to each side. Anything between the two trim calipers will be included in the video.

    To edit another scene, simply click on it and select the *Video Toolbox* again.

7. When finished, click on the "X" in the top right of the window or deselect the **Video Toolbox** button to exit the toolbox.

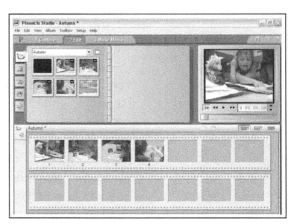

Figure 3.14: Storyboard Scenes

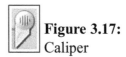

Figure 3.15: Icon Tools

Figure 3.16 Trimming

Figure 3.17: Caliper

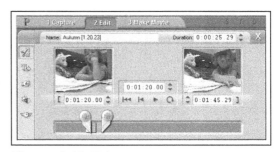

Figure 3.18: Trim

8. Note: If you make a mistake, select **Ctrl + Z** to undo the previous action or click on the **Undo** button in the top-right corner of the screen. To the right of the **Undo** button are the **Redo** and **Help** buttons.

Figure 3.19: Icon Undo

Adding Graphics

1. Adding a still image or images to a video using Studio 8 is a relatively easy task. To add images, begin by selecting **Album > Photos,** or click on the **Frame Grabber** button.

   If all of the graphics intended for use in the video are in a single folder, click on the **Folder** button.

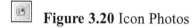

Figure 3.20 Icon Photos

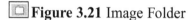

Figure 3.21 Image Folder

   After locating the *Pictures* folder in the *Student of the Week* folder on the Desktop, press **Open**. The individual image files are automatically placed into the *Album* and are easily accessible.

2. To place an image into the video, repeat the process used for inserting video scenes. Select the image and drag it onto the *Storyboard*. To change the order of the images and scenes on the *Storyboard*, simply select and drag to the desired location. For the "Student of the Week" video, here is a recommended order: title scene, scene with the first name and portrait of our "Student of the Week," video of the student interview, images of her artwork, a scene listing her favorite things, video of her drawing, and an end scene.

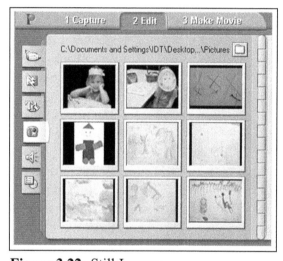

Figure 3.22: Still Images

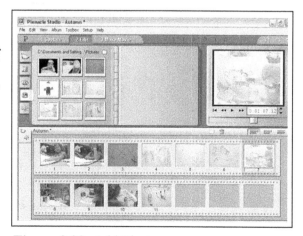

Figure 3.23: Add Photos

Adding Text

1. After all of the scenes and images are in place, insert the titles. There are many different title styles to choose from in Studio 8. To view these styles, click the **Add Title** button on the left side of the *Album*.

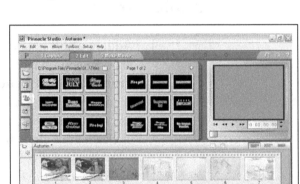

Figure 3.24: Title Icon

To assist in selecting the right one, double click on a title style and it will be illustrated in the *Preview* window. Click on the arrow in the top right of the *Album* to view more title styles.

2. Create a new style or click on a preset style from the *Album*. Select **Toolbox > Create Title**. In this example, create a new style. The beginning title will be on its own background rather than on an image or scene from a video. To do this, select the **Full Screen Title** button.

The title area works differently for versions 8 and 7. Note the directions for the different versions that follow.

Figure 3.25: Titles

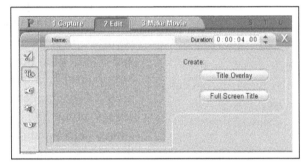

Figure 3.26: Title

- **8.0**
1. Select **Comic Sans MS, 100** point font from the top of the screen. Click in the center of the screen and type "Student." Highlight the word "Student" and then click on the **Looks** button next to the font size indicator. Holding the cursor over the font styles on the far right will showcase a number. In this example, we chose #29-7.

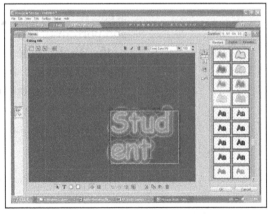

Figure 3.27: Typeface for Studio Version 8.0

2. Click directly on the box around the word "Student" to bring up the resize handles. Drag the handles inwards or outward to fit the text. Select the green rotate handle at the top of the text box and drag it up and to the left to tilt the text box.

3. Move the cursor over the edges of the text box until it turns into a four-headed arrow. Then press and drag it to the top left of the screen.

4. Click off of the text box to deselect it. Change the font size to **60**. Then click on the **Add Text Field** button (the button with the T) located at the bottom of the screen. Click on the bottom of the screen and type "of the week ..." Select **OK** (bottom right of screen) and drag and drop the title at the beginning of the video in the *Storyboard*.

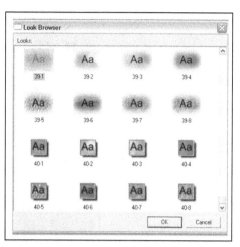

Figure 3.28: Look Browser

- **7.0**

1. To find an appropriate font, select **View > Typeface Browser** to view the available fonts. Select a font and press **OK**. (We chose **Comic Sans MS**.)

2. To set the "look" of the slide, select **View > Look Browser** and select a style. Press **OK**. (We chose look 29-7.) Type "Student of the week..."

3. To change the size of the font, press the up or down arrows to the left of the **Typeface Browser** button (top of the *TitleDeko* window). Other options such as bold, italic, and underline are at the top of the *TitleDeko* window. The center and left alignment options are along the left.

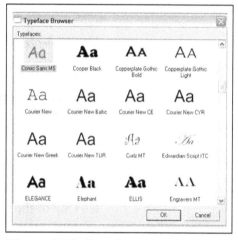

Figure 3.29: Typefaces for Studio Version 7

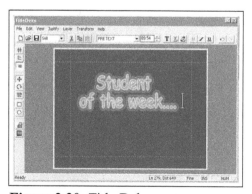

Figure 3.30: Title Deko

4. Highlight "Student" with the mouse by sliding the mouse across the word and select the **Rotate** tool to tilt the text.

   With the **Rotate** tool selected, move the mouse up or down inside the selected text to rotate the word "Student." Click on the **Enable Moving** button.

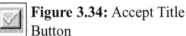 **Figure 3.31:** Rotate Tool

Figure 3.32: Four-Headed Arrow

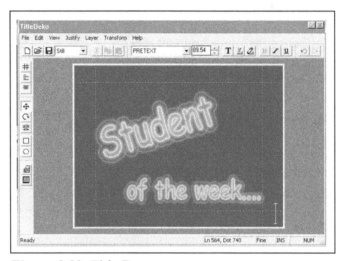

Figure 3.33: Title Done

5. Finally, click on the **Accept Title** button in the top-right corner of the screen and drag and drop the title at the beginning of the video in the *Storyboard*.

 Figure 3.34: Accept Title Button

Adding Music, Narration, and Sounds

1. One of the most important aspects of any video is the audio accompaniment. Fortunately, Studio 8 makes the task of adding sound to a video a very painless process. To view the sound options, click on the **Audio Toolbox** button at the left side of the *Timeline*. The *Audio Volume* window should appear.

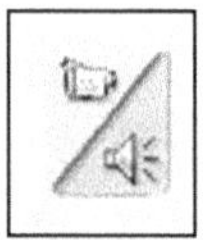

Figure 3.35: Audio Tool

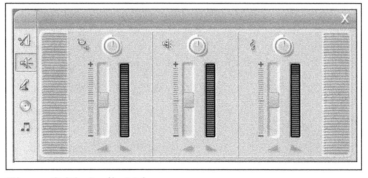

Figure 3.36: Audio Volume

2. Several new buttons are on the left side. These represent individual options for:

  • changing properties of a selected sound clip,

 Figure 3.37: Sound Properties Icon

  • adjusting the volume of a sound file,

 Figure 3.38: Volume Icon

  • recording a new sound file with a computer microphone,

 Figure 3.39: Record New Sound Icon

  • adding a sound file from a CD, and finally,

 Figure 3.40: Add Sound from CD Icon

  • inserting background music automatically.

 Figure 3.41: Insert Background Music Icon

Click on each button to become familiar with the options available for adding and adjusting sound in the video.

3. For the "Student of the Week" video, add some soft piano music to play when the video starts and during the final scene when the student is drawing a picture. Click on the **Create background music automatically** button and use the **Preview** button to sample the music (bottom left of the *Preset Sound Files* window). We selected "Piano Sonata" (the Parlor Piano version). To add the song to the video, simply press the **Add to Movie** button in the middle of the window.

Figure 3.42: Preset Sounds

4. To move the sound file to its proper place in the video, click the **Background Music Track** button and drag the sound clip into the audio track line.

    Continue moving the cursor over the sound file until it turns into a hand. When it turns into a **Hand** button, click and drag the sound anywhere **Figure 3.43:** Background Music Audio Icon along the track so it rests directly beneath the desired point of the video. To shorten or expand the music clip, move the cursor above one end of the clip until the cursor turns into a two-headed arrow; then press the cursor down while moving the end of the clip backward or forward. View the movie by clicking the **Play** button on the movie screen.

5. To fade in the piano music at the beginning, highlight the sound file and move the mouse to the beginning of the sound. Move the cursor up and down along the beginning of the sound clip until it changes to a speaker with an arrow. Click on the left mouse button and drag the blue line in the sound file down. Now the line has moved from the middle of the sound file to the bottom.

6. While still displaying the speaker button, move the mouse a little to the right of the sound file's beginning and drag the blue line back up to the middle of the file. With the volume of the sound now adjusted to fade in at the beginning, the line should appear as shown in the image below. Use the mouse in a similar fashion to fade out the end of a sound file or to adjust the volume levels in the middle of the sound if an additional audio track is playing at the same time.

    When it reaches the sound clip, slide the third volume lever up and down to fade or increase the sound. (Note: To adjust the volume while listening and viewing the movie, click on the **Adjust Volume** button; then play the video.)

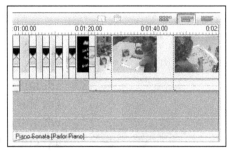

Figure 3.44: Piano File

Figure 3.45: Audio Icon

Adding Transitions

1. Transitions are a visually aesthetic way of blending one film clip or still image into another. Studio comes with a wide variety of transitions. Additional Hollywood-style transitions are also available for purchase. To view the transitions provided with the Studio software, select the **Transition** button at the left of the *Album*.

   To view a demo of the **Transition** effect, click on a transition and it will be demonstrated to the right in the *Preview* window.

 Figure 3.46: Transition Icon

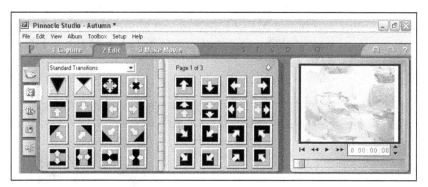

Figure 3.47: Transitions

2. To add a transition between two clips in the video, click on the transition; drag it so it rests between the two clips and let go. To view the transition in the video, select the clip before the transition and click on the **Play** button at the bottom of the *Preview* window. (Note: If the transition fails to apply, be sure the clip is not locked. If it is locked, click on the **Video Camera** button to the left of the *Timeline* to unlock the clip.)

   If unhappy with the look of the transition, simply highlight the transition and press the **Delete** key on the keyboard.

 Figure 3.48: Play Icon

Figure 3.49: Transition Balloon

Exporting the Video

1. Studio offers several formats to export a finished video. These formats include AVI and MPEG. (Version 8 also exports to DVD.) Exporting video is referred to as "making the movie." Select the **Make Movie** tab at the top left of the screen. On the left side of the window, there are the separate file format buttons. To upload the "Student of the Week" video onto the school's Web site, choose the **Stream** button. However, to view the finished video using the computer's media player, choose **MPEG** instead. An alternative way of doing this is selecting **Setup > Make MPEG file**.

Figure 3.50: Make MPEG File

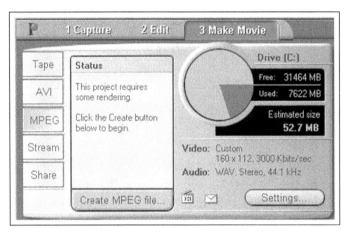

Figure 3.51: Make Movie

2. To change resolution and data rate settings, select the **Settings** button. For this example, choose **MPEG2** in the **Compression** box, change the width and height setting to 720 × 480, and press **OK** to accept the custom setting.

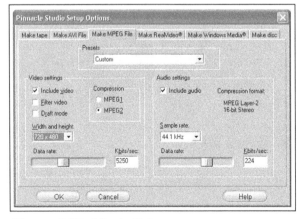

Figure 3.52: Movie Setup

3. Finally, select the **Create MPEG file** button and choose a destination and file name for the video; then press **OK**.

In the *Player* window, notice the **Progress Bars** at the bottom of the window. The bar on top represents how much of the individual clip has been saved, while the bar on the bottom shows how much of the entire movie has been saved.

Figure 3.53: Create MPEG

Figure 3.54: Movie Bars

Export Table for a video approximately 2 minutes and 10 seconds in length:

FORMAT	SIZE	RESOLUTION	PLAYBACK	COMMENTS
AVI	464.8 MB*	720 × 480	Any PC	Large File Size
MPEG1	24.4 MB*	160 × 112	On most players	Small File Size
MPEG2	52.7 MB*	352 × 480	Special player needed	Better Quality than MPEG 1
RealVideo	21.7 MB*	320 × 480	Real Video Player needed	Streaming for Internet
WIN Streaming Media	7.7 MB*	320 × 480	Windows Media Player needed	Streaming for Internet
VHS	164.7 MB	720 × 480	VCR needed	High quality, anyone with a VCR can view it

Table 3.1: Movie Formats

* Resolution and data rate settings may be adjusted, thus affecting final file size. Access the Help menu or program manual to learn more about these settings.

Adaptations and Extensions

Other Ideas to Explore

- Use Studio to create a weekly newscast.
- Try out Version 8's new DVD options.

Curriculum Connections

- **Science.** Create biographies of famous inventors and scientists.
- **History.** Pick a year in time and explore things that happened around the world.
- **Foreign Language.** Create a National Geographic style videography of cultures, customs, sites, and sounds from students' home countries.
- **Physical Education.** Videotape students swimming. Adjust the speed of the movie to replay the strokes in slow motion and analyze good and bad techniques.
- **Library.** Make a video of students engaged in various steps of the research process with captions to explain how a research project should be conducted.

Resources

- Visit Pinnacle Systems Web site at <http://www.pinnaclesys.com>. Pinnacle's Web site contains a lot of content. Pinnacle Systems can be reached at 1-800-4pinnacle.
- Take a tour of Studio 8 at <http://www.pinnaclesys.com/WebVideo/ studioversion8/flashtour/Studio8_Tour_800.html>.
- Try a free trial download of Studio 7. The trial download does not allow capturing of any video via a video camera, but to get an overview of its features visit: <http://apps.pinnaclesys.com/survey/enter.asp?survey_id=119>.
- Pinnacle's video vignettes are designed to entertain and inform the public about Pinnacle's products. These vignettes contain great ideas for designing and creating personal videos; visit <http://www.pinnaclesys.com/ads/vin/videos/main.html>.

Consent, Request, and Order Forms

We have included examples of parental notification and request forms. When considering putting student information on a CD, a video, or online, parents certainly need to be notified. Many parents today are justifiably concerned with privacy issues and would think it unwise to have personal information about their children included in a class project distributed in the community. Other parents may be concerned with identity theft or may be involved in child custody litigation. Whatever the case, these forms have not been created with legal council. They were developed in the interest of keeping parents notified and were developed to ask for parental permission before beginning a project of this nature. It is our recommendation to remain sensitive to these issues before embarking on a project of this sort.

STUDENT OF THE WEEK NOTICE AND REQUEST FORM (example)*

_____ has been chosen as "Student of the Week" for the week of: _____ He/she will be featured in a short video consisting of a brief interview, showcasing his/her best work.

To assist us in this production, we would appreciate any or all of the following:
(These items will be returned to you.)

* artwork
* photos
* writing samples

_____   _____
(Signature of Parent/Guardian)   (Date)

_____   _____
(Address)   (Phone)

- -
(Cut along dotted line.)

PARENTAL CONSENT AND VIDEO ORDER FORM (example)*

I **will** allow the short video presentation of _____
                                                                        (Name of Student)

(Please check all that apply)

❏   to be put on the school's Web site.

❏   to be put on the school's Web site only with encrypted software.

❏   to be included in a compilation video at the end of the school year.

❏   to be archived and stored in the school's library/media center.

_____   _____
(Signature of Parent/Guardian)   (Date)

Because your child has been chosen as a "Student of the Week," you have the option of buying a copy of the compilation video (to be completed by the end of the school year) featuring every honoree. To reserve your copy, please select the appropriate video storage format and number of copies you would like made. Send total along with this consent/order form in the enclosed envelope. Thank you!

	CD-ROM	DVD	VHS	QUANTITY	TOTAL
Student of the Week Video ($10/copy)					

This permission form is intended to be a guide for obtaining parental assistance and consent for "student of the week" video presentations and is customizable in its entirety.

Glossary

Album: Area at the top of the screen that contains the source materials for your video production.

Capture: Importing video material to your computer.

Compression: Method for making files smaller.

Looks Browser: A section of the title editor album with three sub-sections: Standard, Custom, and Favorites.

MPEG: A compressed audio and video file format.

Storyboard View: One of the three views in the movie window. Shows the order of video scenes and transitions via thumbnail icons.

Timeline View: One of the three views in the movie window. Displays five tracks in relation to the time scale.

Chapter 4

A Powerpoint Book Teaser

The Yucca Principle

Introduction

Digital stories can be used to effectively motivate students to read a required book or text or to illustrate its relevance to their personal lives. In one of my courses, students use Robin Williams' *The Non-Designer's Design Book* (Peachpit Press, Inc.) to learn basic design principles. The author's premise is that before you can control the design principles, you need to be able to name them. She gives a personal example of living in a house for 13 years without ever seeing the Joshua trees in her front yard. After receiving a tree identification book as a gift, she became conscious of these trees after she could name them (Williams, pp.1–2). A few weeks after reading this first chapter, a similar incident happened to me. My daughter and I were playing soccer in our backyard. She kicked the ball into a plant in our backyard. I'd never seen the plant before. I asked my wife if she had just planted this "plant" that day. She said that the "Yucca" had been in our yard since we moved to this location a couple of years earlier. Because I had no label for the plant, I gave it no conscious attention. After I found out the name of the plant, I became more observant of the Yuccas around the neighborhood. The goal of this book is to teach students basic design principles. They will learn about these principles and will then be able to name and control their application in the design process.

In this chapter we will create a slide show using Microsoft PowerPoint. PowerPoint is the number one presentation software for business and education and is fairly simple to use.

Materials Needed

- Microsoft PowerPoint, version 2002 XP, 2000, or 97
- Digital Pictures (see relevant sections of Chapter 1 and Appendix B)
  - Autumn approaching the soccer ball

Microsoft PowerPoint® is a registered trademark of Microsoft Corporation.

- Autumn next to the soccer ball
- Autumn kicking—no ball in picture
- Sky (image used was taken from Microsoft's Photo Gallery)
- Backyard shot with the Yucca plant
- Close up of the Yucca plant

A Look at the Completed Project

Figure 4.1: Slide 1—Title zooms in, the line wipes right, "YUCCA" zooms in, and the Joshua tree grows using a wipe up effect.

Figure 4.2: Slide 2—Text "boxes in" or "grows and turns."

Figure 4.3: Slide 3—Text "boxes in" or "grows and turns."

Figure 4.4: Slide 4—Ball appears to be kicked up and forward.

Figure 4.5: Slide 5—The balls appears to fly in the air.

Figure 4.6: Slide 6—The ball lands in the plant. (2002 XP: The ball lands and bounces into the plant.)

Figure 4.7: Slide 7— "What is this plant?" and "… appeared in my yard out of no where!" appear on the screen with a click of the mouse.

Microsoft PowerPoint screen shots reprinted by permission from Microsoft Corporation.

Getting Started with a Storyboard

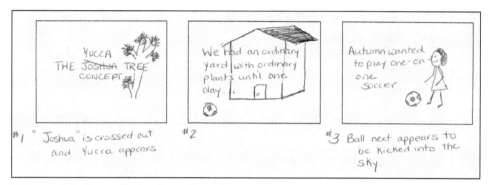

Figure 4.8: PowerPoint Storyboard

Building the Project

1. Open PowerPoint and begin creating the slide show with a blank template.
   [**2000 and 97**: Select **Blank Presentation** in the initial dialog box then **OK**.]

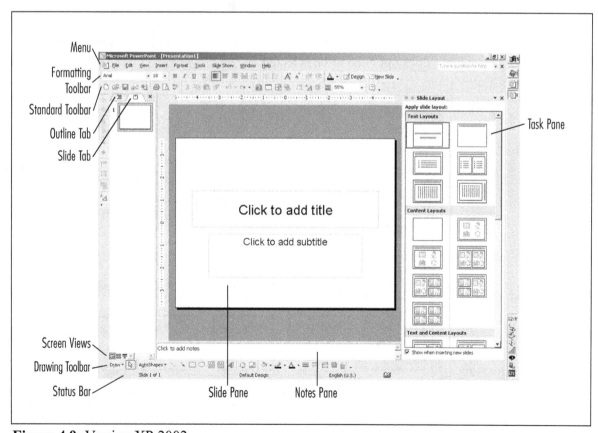

Figure 4.9: Version XP 2002

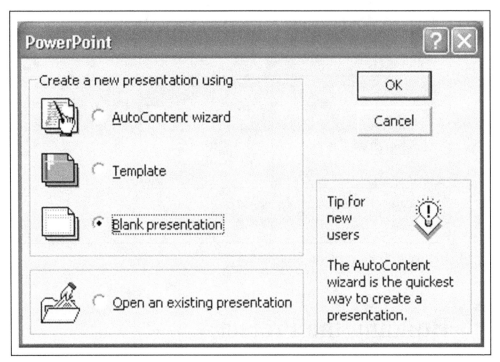

Figure 4.10: Versions 2000 and 97

[**2000 and 97**: Select the **Title Slide** layout in the *New Slide* dialog box; then press **OK**.]

In version XP, the title slide is the default layout for the first slide and does not need to be selected.

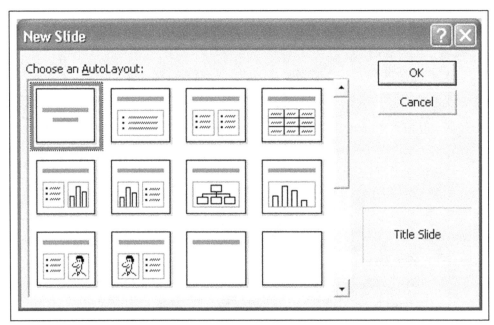

Figure 4.11: Versions 2000 and 97

Select **View > Toolbars** and select the **Format, Standard, Drawing**, and **Task Pane Toolbars**. [**2000 and 97**: There is no *Task Pane* in the earlier versions.]

Creating Customized Backgrounds

1. To create the gradient background on the first slide, select **Format > Background** to bring up the *Background* dialog box.
2. Click on the down arrow next to the long rectangular window. Select **Fill Effects** from the drop-down menu. In the *Fill Effects* dialog box, select the **Gradient** tab.

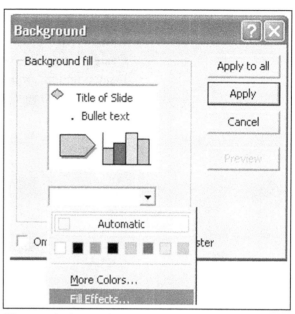

Figure 4.12: Background Dialog Box

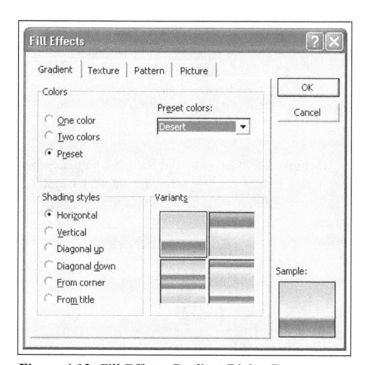

Figure 4.13: Fill Effects Gradient Dialog Box

3. Select **Preset** under *Colors* and click on the down arrow next to the long rectangular window under *Preset Colors*; select **Desert** from the drop-down menu (or create your own gradient by selecting **Two Colors**; then choose a color using the down arrows below *Color 1* and *Color 2*).
4. Press **OK** and the *Background* dialog box will reappear. Click on **Apply** to add the gradient to the first slide only. (**Apply to All** will add the new background to all the slides in the document.)

Creating a Picture Background

1. Click on the **New Slide** button or select **Insert > New Slide** to add a second slide to the slide show. [**2000**: The **New Slide**, **Slide Layout**, and **Apply Design Template** buttons are located under *Common Tasks* on the *Formatting* toolbar.]

Figure 4.14: New Slide Icon

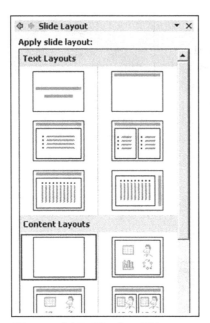

2. Select the **Blank** slide layout under *Content Layouts* in the *Task Pane*.
    [**2000 and 97**: Select the **Blank** slide layout in the *New Slide* dialog box (third row, fourth column).]

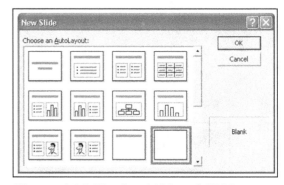

Figure 4.15: Version XP Blank Slide Layout Option

Figure 4.16: Version 2000 and 97 New Slide Dialog Box

3. Select **Format > Background** to bring up the *Background* dialog box.
4. Click on the down arrow next to the long white rectangular window and select **Fill Effects**. The *Fill Effects* dialog box will appear.
5. Click on the **Picture** tab.
6. Press **Select Picture** and locate the picture to be inserted as the background. Click on **Insert**, then **OK**. When the *Background* dialog box reappears, choose **Apply** (not **Apply to All**). [**Version 97**: Once the picture is located click **OK**, then **OK** again.]
    Add the picture backgrounds to the remaining five slides by repeating steps 1–6 for each picture.

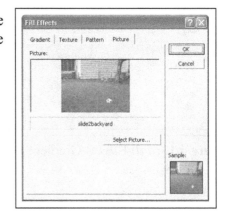

Figure 4.17: Fill Effects Picture Tab

Figure 4.18: Slides 1–7 Without Graphics

Moving and Deleting Slides

Use the **Slide Sorter View** at the bottom of the screen to view all the slides. In version 2002 XP, the *Slide Pane* can also be used to view, arrange, delete, and add slides. **Figure 4.19:** Slide Sorter View Icon

1. Drag and drop any slide to a new location. Click on the slide and the border around the slide will darken. Hold down the mouse while dragging the slide to a new location.

2. A thin vertical line will appear, indicating the new position for the slide. Release the mouse and the slide will appear in the new spot. To delete a slide, *right* click on the slide and select **Delete Slide** or **Cut** from the drop-down menu.

Figure 4.20: Screen with Slides

Adding and Modifying Text

1. Double click on the first slide and click on the top text box and type "THE JOSHUA TREE CONCEPT."

2. Highlight the title by positioning the cursor in front of the first letter of the title. Hold down the mouse while dragging the cursor across the text; then release the mouse.

Figure 4.21: Slide 1 Finished

3. In the *Formatting* toolbar, click on the down arrow next to the first two windows to change the font type and enlarge the font size. (Pictured is the **Showcard Gothic** font at font size **44**.) Also select the **Align Left** button.

Figure 4.22: Formatting Toolbar

Adding Text Boxes and Font Color

1. Add the word "YUCCA" above the word "JOSHUA" by selecting the **Text Box** button on the *Drawing* toolbar (bottom of screen). The cursor will turn into an up-side-down cross.

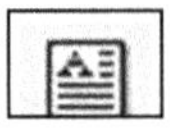

    Figure 4.23: Text Box Button

2. Place the cross above the word "JOSHUA" and press and release the mouse button. A small rectangular text box will form and will enlarge as you type. Type the word "YUCCA." [**97**: Adjust the size of the text box to fit the text.]

3. Change the font type and size to match the font and size of the word "JOSHUA."

4. With the type still selected, change the font color by pressing the down arrow next to the **Font Color** button on the *Drawing* toolbar (bottom of screen) and select a color that compliments the gradient background.

   Figure 4.24: Font Color Button

Rotating Objects

1. To rotate the text, click anywhere inside the "YUCCA" text box to select it. On the *Drawing* toolbar, select **Draw > Rotate** or **Flip > Free Rotate**. [**2000 and 97**: The **Free Rotate** button is located on the *Drawing* toolbar.]

   Figure 4.25: Free Rotate Button

   Small green circles appear at each of the four corners of the text box.

2. Press down on the bottom-left circle and drag the mouse downward to tilt the text box.

3. To move the text box into place, move the cursor over the text box until it turns into a four-sided arrow. At that point, press and drag the mouse to move the box.

Figure 4.26: Yucca Rotated

Working with Lines

1. To add a line across the word "JOSHUA," click on the **Line** button on the *Drawing* toolbar. The cursor will turn into a plus sign when moved over the slide.

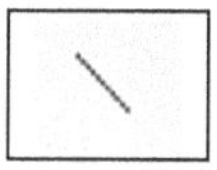

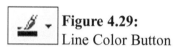

Figure 4.27: Line Button

2. Position the cross at the start of the word "JOSHUA" and drag it across the word; then release the mouse. If the text box interferes with the line, create the line above the text box; then drag it to the desired location. To resize or move an end of a line, select the line and drag a circle or square while at the end of the line to the desired spot.

3. With the line still selected, click on the **Line Style** button on the *Drawing* toolbar and select **4¹/2 pt.** from the drop-down menu to thicken the line.

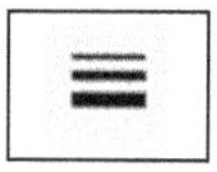

Figure 4.28: Line Style Button

4. Click on the drop-down arrow next to **Line Color** button and select the same color used in the word "YUCCA."

Figure 4.29: Line Color Button

Add the text as shown in slides 2, 3, 4, and 7 using text boxes. The font used in the figures is **Arial Black** set at font size **32–36**.

Figure 4.30: Slide 2 — We had an ordinary yard with ordinary plants until one day ...

Figure 4.31: Slide 3 — Autumn wanted to play one-on-one soccer.

Figure 4.32: Slide 4 — She charged the ball, kicking it high into the sky.

Figure 4.33: Slide 7 — Three text boxes: "What was even more amazing was this plant" "What is this plant?" "... appeared in my yard from no where"

Adding Graphics

2002 XP

1. Navigate to the first slide the select **Insert > Picture > Clip Art** or press the **Clip Art** button.
2. The **Insert Clip Art** menu will appear in the *Task Pane* window. Type "tree" in the *Search text* window.
3. Select the type of file you are looking for by clicking on the down arrow in the *Results should be* window. The *Task Pane* will "fill" with all of the images found. Press **Search**.
4. Click on an image to insert it on the slide.
5. To change or modify the clip art search, press **Modify** at the bottom of the *Task Pane*. To search for more images on Microsoft's Web site, click on the words **Clips Online** (bottom of *Task Pane*).

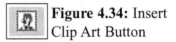

Figure 4.34: Insert Clip Art Button

Figure 4.35: Version XP Clip Art Task Pane

2000

1. Navigate to the first slide; then select **Insert > Picture > Clip Art** or press the **Insert Clip Art** button on the *Drawing Toolbar* to bring up the *Insert Clip Art* dialog box.

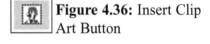

Figure 4.36: Insert Clip Art Button

2. Type "tree" in the *Search for Clips* window and press **Enter**.
3. Click on an image to select it.
4. Click on the image again to bring up the drop-down menu.
5. Press the **Insert Clip** button to insert the image onto the slide.

97

1. Navigate to the first slide; then select **Insert > Picture > Clip Art** or press the **Insert Clip Art** on the *Drawing Toolbar*.
2. Click on **Find** in the *Gallery* box to open the *Find Clip* dialog box.

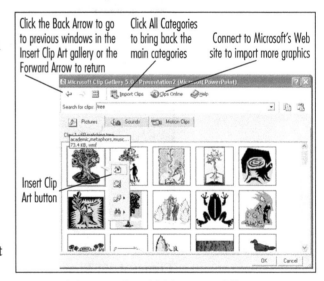

Figure 4.37: Version 2000 Insert Clip Art

3. Type "tree" in the *Keywords* window and press **Find Now**.
4. Double click on any image to insert it on the slide.

Images from the Web

Microsoft's clip art gallery is limited. However, with Internet access, Microsoft's Design Gallery Live has a vast archive of downloadable images available for use with PowerPoint.

1. Connect to the Internet. Select **Insert > Picture > Clip Art** or press the **Insert Clip Art** button.
2. Press the **Clips Online** button (the button with the globe) in the *Insert Clip Art Task Pane* or dialog box. Your browser will open Microsoft's Design Gallery Live Web site <dgl.microsoft.com>.
3. Choose **Accept**, after reading Microsoft's licensing agreement, to get access to the site.
4. Type "tree" in the *Search for* window and press **Enter**.
5. Select the desired image(s) by checking the small box below the thumbnail picture(s). A "download" hyperlink will appear above the image(s). Select it. A new Web page appears.
6. Press the **Download Now** link to download the images into your *Insert Clip Art Task Pane* or dialog box.
7. Close the *Insert Clip Art* window.
8. Close the Internet window(s).
9. Tip: To use online images from Microsoft's Web site as a slide background, create a folder on the Desktop to save images. Once the desired image is located, click on the image for a "Live Preview." A box will appear with the image enlarged. *Right* click on the picture and select **Save Target As** from the drop-down menu. In the *Save Picture* dialog box, rename the image and save it to the folder on the Desktop.

Inserting an Image from a Location Other than Microsoft

Figure 4.38: Slide 1

1. Press **Insert > Picture > From File**.
2. Locate the image in the *Insert Picture* dialog box and give it a name; then press **Insert**.

    Slide 1: Insert an image of a tree to the right of the title. (Slides 2, 3, and 7 contain no clip art.)

    Slide 4: Insert an image of a ball as shown.

Figure 4.39: Slide 4—One Ball

A. To create the illusion of continuous motion, only one ball is needed for the animation effect in version 2002 XP. (If you were unable to find a ball, add a circle by clicking on the **Oval** button on the *Drawing Toolbar*. The cursor will turn into cross hairs. With **Shift** selected on the keyboard, press down on the mouse and drag the cursor on the screen.)

B. For **2000 and 97**, additional balls must be added. Here's how:

i. To make additional balls, select the ball on the screen and click on **Edit > Copy** or click on the **Copy** button. Next select **Edit > Paste** or click on the **Paste** button. A second ball will appear on the screen. Enlarge the ball slightly (holding down the **Shift** key will retain the image's proportions); then position it slightly above the first ball.

 Figure 4.40: Cut, Copy, and Paste Buttons.

Figure 4.41: Slide 4— Two Balls

ii. Select **Edit > Paste** again. Enlarge the ball slightly and position it into place.

iii. Continue adding balls to the slide until they appear to "fly" off the screen. Adding the balls in a consecutive sequence will make animating the objects easier.

Figure 4.42: Slide 4— Many Balls

Slide 5

A. **2002 XP**: Add one soccer ball off to the bottom left of the screen.

B. **2000 and 97**: Use the cut and paste method to add the balls from left to right as shown.

Figure 4.43: Slide 5— Position ball slightly below the screen for version 2002 XP.

Figure 4.44: Slide 5— Position of balls for versions 2000 and 97.

Slide 6

A. **2002 XP**: Add one ball above the slide as illustrated.

B. **2000 and 97**: Using the cut and paste method, create a path of balls starting from the top of the screen and extending to the yucca.

Figure 4.45: Slide 6—Position of ball slightly above the slide for version 2002 XP.

Figure 4.46: Slide 6—Position of balls for versions 2000 and 97.

Adding Custom Animation Effects

<u>2002 XP</u>

Slide 1

1. Navigate to the title slide.

2. Select **Slide Show > Custom Animation**. The *Custom Animation* menu may appear in the *Task Pane* window on the right side of the screen or as a floating box.

3. Select the title on the slide; then press **Add Effect**.

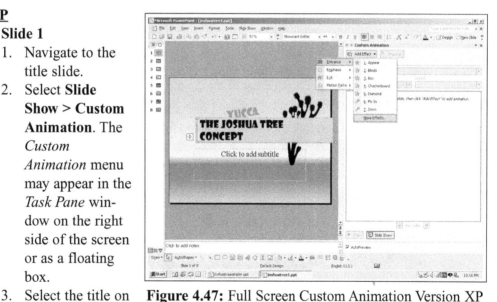

Figure 4.47: Full Screen Custom Animation Version XP

Select **Entrance** from the drop-down menu. (**Entrance** refers to animation effects applied to objects as they first appear on the slide.) The most recently/commonly used effects will appear in the drop-down menu. Choose **Zoom** from the drop-down menu. If it is not listed in the drop-down list, select **More Effects** at the bottom of the drop-down menu; then scroll down and select **Zoom** and **OK**.

4. Click anywhere outside the title area to deselect the title. Then select the line and click on **Add Effect** and select **Entrance** from the menu. Click on **Wipe**. If it is not listed in the drop-down box, click on **More Effects** and scroll to find it. To change the direction of the animation, use the down arrow in the *Direction* window and select **From Left** in the drop-down menu.
5. Select the word "YUCCA" on the slide and add the entrance effect **Zoom**.
6. Select the graphic of the tree and add the entrance effect **Wipe**. Change the direction of the animation to **From Bottom**. Click on the **Play** button to preview all the animation effects on the slide. If you make a mistake, simply select an object on the slide and press the **Remove** button (top of *Task Pane*) in the *Custom Animation* window. Animation effects associated with the object will be removed.

Slides 2 and 3
Select the text on the slide and select **Entrance > Grow and Turn**.

Slide 4
1. Click on the graphic of the ball and add an **Emphasis** effect. (**Emphasis** refers to an animation effect applied to an object that is already on the screen when played in *Slide Show View*.) Select **Grow/Shrink** and use the down arrow under **Speed** to select **Fast**.
2. Click on the down arrow at the far right of the *Task Pane* and select **Effect Options** from the drop-down menu.
   Under *Settings*, use the down arrow to select the size **Huge**. Next to the *Sound* window, use the down arrow to select **Whoosh**. Press **OK**.

Figure 4.48: Slide 4—Custom Animation Effects Version XP

Slide 5
A motion path will be used to create the illusion of the ball flying in air.
1. Select the ball and then choose **Motion Paths** as the animation effect. Select **Draw Custom Path > Curve**.
2. Click on the ball to begin the path. Click on the middle of the slide near the top (this will be the apex of the path where the ball begins to

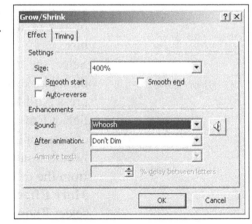

Figure 4.49: Custom Animation Effects Version XP

decline); then double click below the slide on the right side to end the path. The ball will follow the arched path. Notice the path on the slide. The green arrow indicates the beginning of the path and the red arrow signals the end.

3. Adjust the speed of the animation using the *Speed* window.

Slide 6

1. Select the ball and add the **Motion Paths** effect. Select **Draw > Custom Path > Freeform**.
2. Start the path by clicking once on the ball.
   You can direct the line by clicking on the slide, creating a path for the line. Make the ball fall into the Yucca plant and bounce up once or twice before resting in the plant. Double click to end the line.
3. Edit the path by *right* clicking on it and choose **Edit Points** from the drop-down menu.
4. Edit the points by dragging them to the desired position.

Figure 4.50: Slide 5—Ball Path

Slide 7

1. Do not animate the first text box.
2. Select the words "What is this plant?" and add the **Entrance** effect **Appear**.
3. Select the words "... appeared in my yard out of no where!" and select **Appear**.

2000 and 97

1. Navigate to the first slide.
2. Select **Slide Show > Custom Animation**. The *Custom Animation* dialog box will appear.
3. Click on the **Order and Timing** or **Timing** tab.
4. Click on the little box next to Title 1 in the *Check to animate slide objects* window. Next select the line, the text "YUCCA," and the picture for animation. [**97**: Click on the title in the *Slide objects without animation* window and check **Animate**. Do the same for the line, the text "YUCCA," and the picture.]

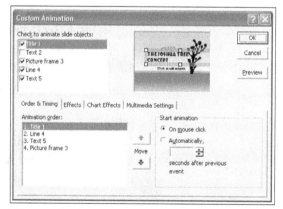

Figure 4.51: Custom Animation Title 1

5. The title, line, text, and picture are now listed in the *Animation Order* window. Change the order of the animations by using the up and down arrows.

6. Select the **Effects** tab. Highlight Title 1 in the top-left window and select **Zoom In** under *Entry animation and sound*.

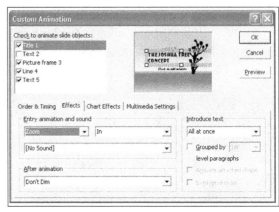

Figure 4.52: Custom Animation Effects Tab

7. Highlight the **Line** in the *Animation* window and choose **Wipe Right** as the animation effect. Use the animation **Zoom In** for the text "YUCCA" and **Wipe Up** for the picture frame (Yucca graphic).

8. Click on **Preview** to see how these animations will play in the *Preview* window. Make adjustments in the **Order and Timing** tab (or **Timing** tab) or with the **Effects** tab. When satisfied press **OK**.

Slides 2 and 3

1. Select **Slide Show > Custom Animation** to bring up the *Custom Animation* dialog box.
2. Select the text on the slide and select **Box out** as the animation effect in the **Effects** tab.
3. Click on the **Preview** button to view the animation; then press **OK**.

Slides 4, 5, and 6

1. Select **Slide Show > Custom Animation**.
2. Select the objects you wish to animate. Make sure the balls are in the correct animation order in the **Order and Timing** tab or **Timing** tab and for each ball choose *Start Animation Automatically 0 seconds after previous event*.
3. In the **Effects** tab, select **Appear** as the animation effect for each of the balls. Also, in the *After Animation* window, choose **Hide After Animation**.
4. Preview the animation before pressing **OK** to be sure that you have created the desired animation effects.

Slide 7

Do not select an animation effect for the text "What was more amazing was that this plant ..." Select **Appear** for the text "What is this plant?" and "... appeared in my yard out of no where!"

Viewing the Final Slide Show

1. Navigate to the first slide and select the **Slide Show View** button to see the full slide show on a full screen.

Figure 4.53: Slide Show View Button

2. To advance the slides, press the mouse button or **Enter** on the keyboard. (Troubleshooting: If the animations do not play, click on **Slide Show > Set up Slide Show**. Deselect **Show without animation** and press **OK**.)
3. Click on **Esc** on the keyboard to exit the show at any time.

Adaptations and Extensions

Other Ideas to Explore

- If version 2002 XP was used to create the "Yucca Principle" slide show, consider integrating it into Microsoft Producer. Producer is a free program available for download from Microsoft's Web site.
- If your computer has a microphone and speakers, why not add personal narration to your slides? Select **Slide Show > Record Narrations**. Select the desired recording quality and press **OK**. When the first slide appears, talk into the microphone to begin the narration. Press **Enter** to bring up the next animation or slide and to establish optional automatic timings for your slides.
- Add hyperlinks to additional sources of information on the Web, to an e-mail address, to other slides in the slide show, or to other files. Hyperlinks can be added to text, graphics, and buttons to play a sound or to run a macro or an action. Select an object on a slide and press the **Insert Hyperlink** button on the *Standard toolbar* or choose **Slide Show > Action Settings**. Add a quick button by going to **Slide Show > Action Buttons**.

Curriculum Connections

The format used in the "Yucca" slide show can be used to motivate students to read a book in nearly any subject area. Here are few examples:

- **Library Media Specialist**. Find a short, interesting segment from a book and integrate it with a personal story or example to pique the listener's interest in reading the book.
- **Math**. Develop a digital story to illustrate a story problem or to generate a discussion for a mathematical solution.
- **Science**. Encourage students to read books about science, such as Stephen Hawking's *A Brief History of Time*, by illustrating a short segment of the book.
- **Physical Education**. Use Aesop's fable *The Tortoise and the Hare* to portray the importance of pacing one's self and continual persistence.
- **General**. Create a story about a day in the life of a student.

Resources

- PowerPoint in the Classroom is a great step-by-step tutorial produced by Act360 Media Ltd in conjunction with Microsoft PowerPoint; visit <http://www.actden.com/pp>.
- Microsoft's Web site has an extensive archive of clip art, design templates, tips and tricks, tutorials, and downloads for PowerPoint and is a must for PowerPoint users; visit <http://www.microsoft.com/office/powerpoint>.
- Learn how to effectively animate graphs and to create custom templates and advanced animation features and ways to use PowerPoint in the classroom at <http://www.solida.net/powerpoint>.
- This extensive tutorial for PowerPoint version 2000 is produced by Florida Gulf Coast University; visit <http://www.fgcu.edu/support/office2000/ppt>.
- Frequently asked questions, keyboard shortcuts, and PowerPoint tips and tricks are featured on A Bit Better Corporation's Web site: <http://www.bitbetter.com/powertips.htm>.
- Two general sources for articles related to presentations include Presenters University's Web site: <http://www.presentersuniversity.com/index.cfm> and Presentations.com: <http://www.presentations.com/presentations/index.jsp>. Presenters University is also a terrific source for design templates.
- To access Microsoft PowerPoint's **Help** menu, select **Help > Microsoft PowerPoint Help**. The Office Assistant will appear (normally in the form of an animated paperclip). Click on the Office Assistant and type a question or phrase for personal assistance.

Glossary

Clips Online: A button in the clip art window that allows users to access Microsoft's extensive online gallery for thousands of images, sounds, and pictures.

Design Template: A specially designed slide background.

Emphasis Effect: An animation effect applied to an object that is already on the screen when played in slide show view in XP only.

Entrance Effect: Animation effects applied to objects as they first appear on the slide.

Fill: Coloring inside a shape or image using the paint bucket.

Formatting Toolbar: Contains tools for formatting, or altering, the way text looks.

Motion Path: An animation effect that creates the illusion of an object following a path in XP only.

Office Assistant: An animated character (normally a paper clip) on the screen that can provide tips and help as you work with the program.

Slide Layout: A template that places text, pictures, and graphs on specific areas of the slide and automatically resizes them.

Standard Toolbar: Located at the top of the screen, it contains a row of buttons or icons for performing common tasks such as printing and opening files.

Task Pane: A new feature in version XP. It is a context sensitive area on the right side of the screen that contains the tools and menus needed to perform tasks.

Chapter 5

A Biography in Premiere

Churchill's Guardian Angel

Introduction

In this chapter, students will utilize Adobe Premiere, a video-editing software program, to learn advanced techniques for presenting a digital biography. Upon completion of their digital biographies, students should begin to realize there is more than one way to tell a story. It is important to note that Adobe Premiere is a very robust video-editing tool and that the following instructions are offered as an introductory guide for utilizing the program to develop a relatively simple digital story.

For over 50 years, the touching story of a chance meeting between Winston Churchill and Alexander Fleming has enjoyed countless retellings in books, newspapers, magazines, and, most recently, on the Internet. Though there are some sources that assert the story is more fiction than fact, it is, nevertheless, an inspirational tale. There are many versions of the tale, three of which are cited in the final bullet of the "Resources" section to this chapter, but the essence of it is as follows:

> While vacationing in Scotland, a young British boy wanders away from his parents and ends up finding himself in quite a predicament. Struggling to stay afloat in an isolated pond, he cries out for help. Working in a field close by, the son of a Scottish farmer hears his cries and saves him from drowning. As one may imagine, the father of the British boy was very appreciative and wanted to repay the Scottish lad for saving his son's life. Therefore, after finding out the boy dreamed of studying medicine and becoming a doctor, he offered to pay for the boy's entire education. Many years later, in the winter of 1943, Winston Churchill became very ill while in North Africa. Sir Alexander Fleming flew from England to administer penicillin, a drug he had recently discovered, to Churchill in hopes of curing his ailment. The miracle drug worked. Alexander Fleming had succeeded in saving Churchill's life a second time, for it was he that had rescued Winston Churchill from drowning decades before.

Materials Needed

- Adobe Premiere 6.0 or 5.1
- Multimedia-enabled computer with microphone and IEEE 1394/FireWire inputs
- Video camera with IEEE 1394/FireWire computer-enabled equipment or cables
- Microphone
- Seven digital pictures and a one-minute video clip (Note: This project may be completed successfully without video, using just the digital pictures.)

A Look at the Completed Project

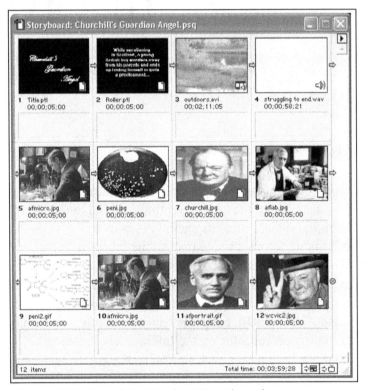

Figure 5.1: Completed Project Storyboard

Adobe® Premiere® screen shots reprinted with permission from Adobe Systems, Inc. Adobe Premiere is a registered trademark of Adobe Systems Incorporated in the United States and other countries.

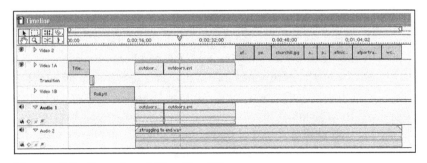

Figure 5.2: Completed Timeline View

Getting Started with a Storyboard

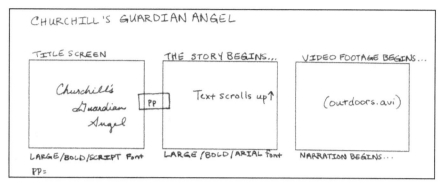

Figure 5.3: Storyboard

Building the Project

1. Prepare materials for this project by taking one or two minutes of video of a pond or small lake. Also, surf online and download seven images. More specifically, find three images of Alexander Fleming as a doctor, two of an older Winston Churchill, and two images of penicillin. To ensure proper viewing proportions when inserting a graphic into Premiere, it is wise to resize the images, using an image editor, to 720×480 pixels. Create a folder on the Desktop called *Churchill's Guardian Angels*. Create a folder inside this folder called *Images*; this is where you will save the images. For information on finding images online or resizing images using Photoshop Elements, see relevant sections from Appendix B.

2. **6.0**: Open Premiere and begin creating the video as a new project. Select **File > New Project (Ctrl + N** or **F2)** to begin. A window titled *Load Project Settings* appears. **Standard 32kHz** should be highlighted under the folder *DV–NTSC*. Press **OK**.

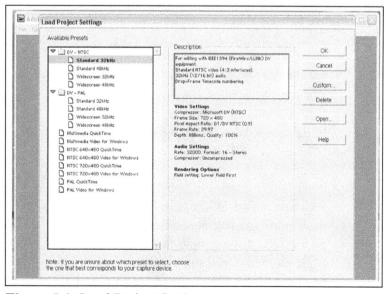

Figure 5.4: Load Project Settings

[**5.1**: Upon opening Adobe Premiere, the *New Projects Settings* window will appear. The project settings will be specified here. In the *General Settings*, make sure that the *Time Display* is set to **30 fps Drop-Frame Timecode**; then click on the **Next** button located on the right-hand side of the window. The window will now move to the *Video Settings*. Set the Compressor as **DV-NTSC**, the Depth to **Millions**, and the Frame Size to **720 h and 480 v**; make sure that the **4:3 Aspect** is selected, the Frame Rate is **29.97**, and the Quality is **100%**. Click on the **Next** button to move to the *Audio Settings*. Here set the Rate as **32 kHz**, the Format as **16 Bit – Stereo**, and the Type as **Uncompressed**. Click on the **Next** button again to move to the *Keyframe and Rendering Options* and set the *Field Setting* to **Lower Field First**. After the proceeding settings have been selected, click on the **OK** button on the upper-right-hand corner of the *New Projects Settings* window.]

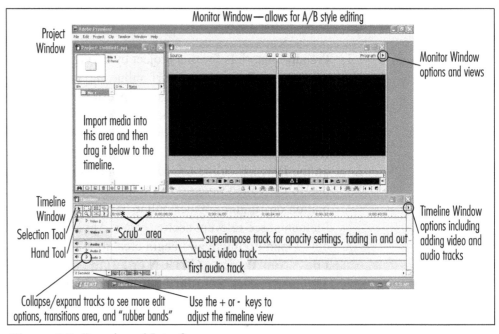

Figure 5.5: Premiere 6 Interface

3. **6.0**: In the *Project* window, *right* click on the smallest folder titled *Bin 1* and select **Rename Bin**. A window named *Bin Alias* will appear. In the text window next to *Bin Name*, type "Churchill." [**5.1**: In this version of Adobe Premiere, a Bin will have to be created before it can be renamed. Begin by choosing **Project > Create > Bin**. When asked for a title, type a word or phrase that concisely describes the project. For this example, we will name the Bin *Churchill*. Once this has been completed double click the Bin so that it is open in the *Project* window.]

Figure 5.6: Project Window

4. This is a good time to save the project. To do so, select **File > Save As** to bring up the *Save File* window. After choosing the *Churchill's Guardian Angel* folder on the Desktop, name the file *Biography* and press **Save**.

5. To adjust the window sizes of the project, Timeline, or other screen areas, so all are visible in a single glance, drag the mouse to any corner or side of each window until the cursor changes to a double arrow icon.

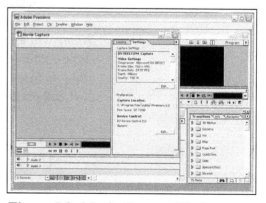

Hold down the mouse button and drag the mouse up or down to adjust the size of the window. Repeat this process for each window until satisfied with its appearance. In addition, it is possible to drag any of the individual windows to any preferred area of the screen as desired. Additional windows may be opened by selecting **Window** on the *Menu Bar*. Selecting, for example, **Window > Show Transitions** will open the *Transitions* window in the bottom-right corner of the screen.

Figure 5.7: Two-Headed Arrow

Capturing Video

1. Connect the FireWire cable to the video camera and the computer. Also, make sure the tape with a two-minute clip of an outdoor pond scene is in the camera. This pond clip will be played in the first part of the video while the narration is beginning. (Note: Video saved as an .avi or .mpeg file can also be imported into the project. Go to **File > Import > File** and locate the video file and press **OK**. Also, Premiere is a great program for just using still pictures when video is not available. This is because effects like panning and zooming on these still images creates the illusion of video movement. When used properly, viewers may not even notice that the entire project was made up of digital pictures.)

2. To start capturing video from the video camera to the computer, select **File > Capture > Movie Capture (F5)**. A window may appear advising the selection of appropriate device settings.

3. **6.0**: Select **Edit Settings** and refer to the Adobe Premiere's accompanying manual for suggestions, or select **OK** to use the default settings. [**5.1**: To change the edit settings move to the toolbar and select **Project > Settings > Capture** and refer to the Adobe Premiere's accompanying manual for suggestions, or select **OK** to use the default settings.]

4. **6.0**: The *Movie Capture* window will appear. Under the **Settings** tab, observe the *Capture Settings* and *Preferences* that will be used to capture video from a video camera. In the *Preferences* box, notice the heading *Capture Location*. This location is where video footage will be saved. Video footage demands a great

Figure 5.8: Movie Capture Window

deal of memory, so make sure the location stated has enough disk space available for capturing the video. If it does not, alter the capture location by clicking the **Edit** button in the *Preferences* box and choose **Select Folder** in the text box next to *Captured Movies* under the heading *Scratch Disks and Device Control*.

[**5.1**: To view the capture set-tings and preferences, again move to **Project > Settings > Capture** and the *Project Settings* dialog box will open in *Capture Settings* mode. To move between the different *Project Settings* modes, click the **Next** button on the right-hand side of the win-dow. To designate where the movie will be saved, move to the

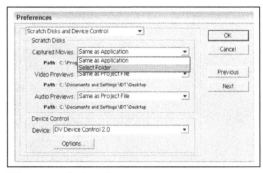

Figure 5.9: Preferences

toolbar and select **File > Preferences > Scratch Disks / Device Controls** and then choose the capture location in this window.]

5. **6.0**: Now, to begin capturing video footage, first make sure the video cam-era is on and set to the VCR or VTR modes. Use either the rewind and fast-forward controls at the bottom of the *Movie Capture* window, or the controls on the video **Figure 5.10:** Rewind
camera itself, to locate the starting point of
the footage that needs to be recorded. **Figure 5.11:** Fast Forward

[**5.1**: VTR and VCR modes are not a function in this version of the program, meaning that the controls on the video camera itself will have to be used to locate and play the video clip.]

6. **6.0**: To begin capturing the footage, click
the **Record** button in the bottom left of the **Figure 5.12:** Record
Movie Capture window.

[**5.1**: The **Record** button is located at the top center of the *Movie Capture* window.]

7. Press the **Escape** key on the keyboard to stop recording after capturing the desired footage. A window labeled *File Name* will appear. Type "outdoors" in the *File Name* dialog box and press **OK**.

Figure 5.13: Record Movie

Figure 5.14: File Name

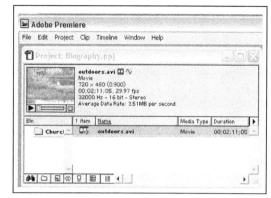

Figure 5.15: Video Bin

8. Close the *Movie Capture* window. The video footage saved is now located in the appropriate Bin with its file name.

Editing the Video Clip

1. Begin editing the *outdoors* footage of the pond by clicking the icon to the left of its file name and dragging the file from the Bin into the *Timeline* window onto the *Video 1* track. [**5.1**: *Video 1A* track.] The sound accompanying the footage will automatically place itself into the *Audio 1* track. In addition to the *Timeline*, the footage is also visible in the *Monitor* window. To view the video at any time, press the **Play** button at the bottom of the *Monitor* window or the **space bar** on the keyboard. (If you are working in dual monitor mode, the preview will occur in the right monitor.) As you play the video, notice the *Edit Line* that moves across the movie clip in the *Timeline* window.

Figure 5.16: Movie Clip Icon

Figure 5.17: Play Button

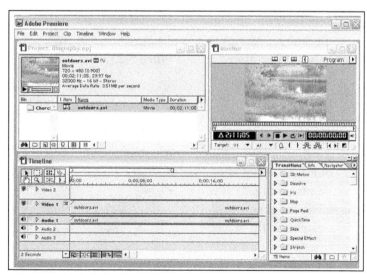

Figure 5.18: Edit Timeline

2. Make sure the yellow bar [**5.1**: purplish-blue bar] at the top of the *Timeline* window stretches to the end of the video. This bar establishes the in and out points of your video.

3. There are many tools to assist in editing the video. Some of these, including the **Arrow**, **Range Select**, and **Razor** tools, may be found in the top left of the *Timeline* area.

4. Scrub the *Timeline* by pressing and dragging the mouse across the numbers in the *Timed Intervals* area at the very top of the *Timeline*. This plays the video clip as fast or as slow as the area is scrubbed. When doing this, as the *Edit Line* moves across the movie clip in the *Timeline* area, watch the video as it plays in the *Monitor* window. Scrubbing is a very useful feature to help quickly assess if there are parts of the clip that need to be separated.

Figure 5.19: Timeline Tools

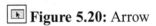 **Figure 5.20:** Arrow

Figure 5.21: Razor

Figure 5.22: Range Select Tool

5. Separate the *outdoors* clip, simply by moving the *Edit Line* to the spot to be split and select the **Razor** tool in the top left of the *Timeline* window. Drag the **Razor** tool over the *Edit Line* in the *Video 1* track. When it is sitting directly on the *Edit Line*, click once on the mouse button. Notice the beveled separation line that appears in both the video and audio tracks. The single clip of video footage has now become two.

6. To delete a section of a clip, drag the *Edit Line* to the beginning point of the section you wish to delete and select the **Razor** tool. Drag the **Razor** tool over the *Edit Line* in the *Video 1* track. When it is sitting directly on the *Edit Line*, click once on the left mouse button. Then drag the *Edit Line* to the ending point of the section you wish to delete and click the **Razor** tool again. Finally, select the **Arrow** tool and click somewhere in the middle of the section to be deleted. Once it is highlighted (with a moving dotted line around it) press the **Delete** key on the keyboard.

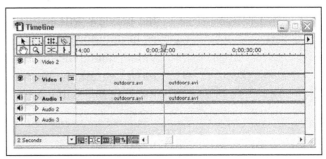

Figure 5.23: Timeline Bevel

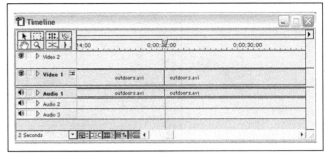

Figure 5.24: Timeline Dotted

7. There is now an empty space in the middle of the movie clip. To close this gap in the video footage, click and drag the clip on the right, to the left, until the vertical line that appeared meets the clip on the left. Next, in the *Scrub* area, drag the *Edit Line* to the left of the beveled separation line. Push the **Play** button in the monitor window, or the **space bar** on the keyboard, to view the newly edited video. Repeat these editing procedures until satisfied with the appearance and continuity of the video footage. Just less than 30 seconds is needed for the introduction. Another short clip could also be used at the conclusion of this story.

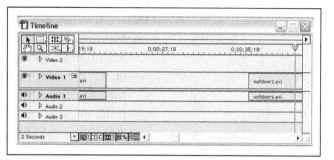

Figure 5.25: Separated Timeline

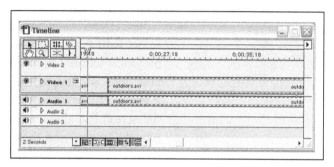

Figure 5.26: Drag Timeline

Adding Graphics

1. Adding a still image or images to video is a relatively easy way to enhance its overall impression. Import graphics into the video project by selecting **File > Import > File (Ctrl + I** or **F3)**. In this case, since all of the graphics intended for use in this project are in the sub-folder titled *Images* within the folder *Churchill's Guardian Angel*, select **File >**

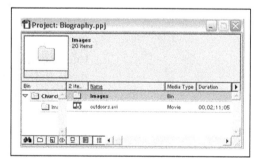

Figure 5.27: Images Folder

Import > Folder (Ctrl + Shift + I or **F4)** instead. After locating the files or folder, press **OK**. Notice the folder or individual image files chosen were automatically placed into the project Bin.

2. Adobe Premiere automatically sets the amount of time, or duration, that a still image will appear in the video. To change the duration of still images imported into Premiere, select **Edit > Preferences > General and Still Image**. [**5.1**: **File > Preferences > General and Still Image**.] In the *Still Image* box at the bottom of the *Preferences* window, change the number of frames per second to alter the duration. For this project, change the frames

from **150** (about five seconds at 29.97 frames per second) to **120** (about four seconds) and press **OK**.

3. Other ways to quickly change the duration of an image are by *right* clicking on the image and selecting **Duration** or by double clicking on the individual image file and clicking on the **Duration** button in the bottom-left-hand corner of the clip. To alter the image's duration, simply type in your preference and press **OK**.

4. Note: If you make a mistake, select **Edit > Undo** to undo the previous action. Or, to undo several actions at once, select **Window > Show History** and simply select the action just above where the mistakes began and the mistakes will be conveniently erased. [**5.1**: This version does not contain a History.]

5. For this example, the images of Winston Churchill and Alexander Fleming will serve to illustrate the story of their momentous meeting. To access these individual image files, double click on the *Images* folder icon in the project Bin so they all are visible in the *Project* window.

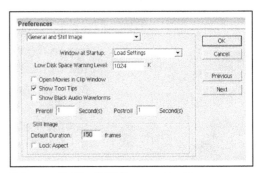

Figure 5.28: Still Image Preferences

Figure 5.29: Duration

Figure 5.30: History 1

Figure 5.31: History 2

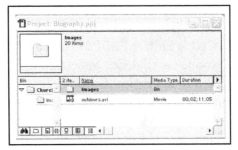

Figure 5.32: Images Folder 2

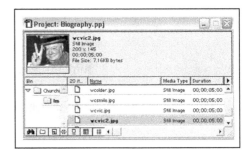

Figure 5.33: Project Window 2

6. To insert one of the images into the *Timeline*, simply click the icon to the left of its file name and drag the file from the Bin into the *Timeline* window onto the *Video 2* track.

When completed, the images will appear after the outdoors video footage and not at the same time. For now, drag the seven images retrieved online for 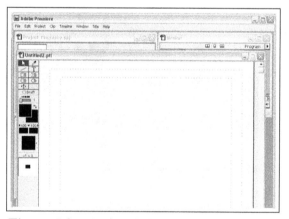 **Figure 5.34:** File

Figure 5.22: Range Select Tool

this project to the right of the 40 second mark and directly next to each other in the following order: Fleming1, Penicillin1, Churchill1, Fleming2, Penicillin2, Fleming 1 (repeated), Fleming3, and Churchill2. To move clips (images, sounds, or video footage), select the **Range Select** tool; then click on a clip to select it. Marching ants will now appear to be moving around the entire clip. Move the cursor inside the box; press and drag the clip to the right or left to move the clip as needed.

7. After all of images for the video are on the *Timeline*, drag the *Edit Line* to the beginning of the video and watch as it moves over the video footage and then the images.

8. **6.0 only**: Another excellent way to add graphics (if the exact position in the Timeline is known for each image) is to move the *Edit Line* to the exact point, click on the image name in the *Project Bin*, and select **Clip > Insert at Edit Line** (**Ctrl + Shift**, or **Shift + F2**).

Adding Titles

1. To add a title to the video, select **File > New > Title** (**F9**). The *Title* window appears. The dotted lines visible in the *Title* window are there for a purpose. The inner dotted line represents the *Title-Safe* area. It is a good idea to keep titles or text within this boundary to enhance the likelihood that they will be readable no matter what size television screen is being used for viewing. The outer dotted line represents the *Action-Safe* area. Graphics or text, in the area within this border, should be viewable on most television screens.

Figure 5.35: Action Safe Area

2. For this example, use white text on a black background. To change the background color from white to black, *right* click in the *Title* window and select **Title Window Options**.

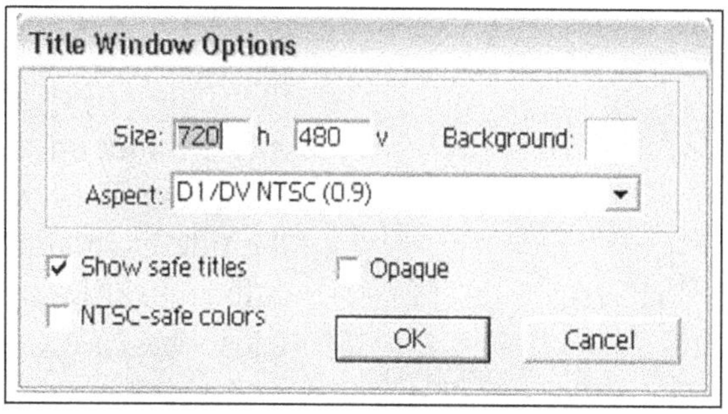

Figure 5.36: Title Window Options

3. After double clicking the **Color** square next to the heading *Background*, the *Color Picker* dialog box should appear. Choose **Black** for the background by clicking in the black area of the *Color Picker* dialog box or by changing the numbers next to *Red*, *Green*, and *Blue* to **0**. Press **OK** and **OK** again to close the *Color Picker* and *Title Window Options* dialog boxes.

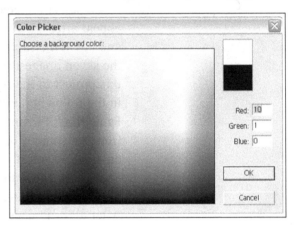

Figure 5.37: Color Picker

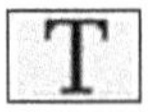

4. The title screen of this video will say *Churchill's Guardian Angel*. Select **Title > Font** to open the *Font* dialog box. Select a script font style such as **Edwardian Script ITC**, **Bold**, and **72** point size and press **OK**. Select the **Text** icon on the left side of the *Title* window; then click inside of the *Title* window area and begin typing.

Figure 5.38: T Icon

To stretch the text box, click on a corner. Grey squares should appear in the four corners of the box. Click on a square and drag to make the writing area larger.

Figure 5.39: Smaller Title

Figure 5.40: Larger Title

5. After typing "Title," save it by selecting **File > Save As**. Name it *Title* and place it in the *Churchill's Guardian Angel* folder on the Desktop and press **Save**. After saving the title, it should automatically appear in the Bin. Close the *Title* window.

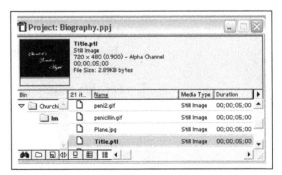

Figure 5.41: Title Bin

6. **6.0**: To place the title in the beginning of the video, move the *Edit Line* to the beginning of the *Timeline*; click on *Title* in the project Bin and select **Clip > Insert at Edit Line** (**Ctrl + Shift + ,** or **Shift + F2**). [**5.1**: To create space at the beginning of the movie, move the existing movie clips to the right with the **Rectangle Select** tool before inserting the clip. Then move the existing clips back to the left until they are in contact with the new title clip.]

7. To play the video and view the new title, the work area must be rendered. **6.0**: A red bar at the top of the *Timeline* window indicates that the section of video containing the new title has not been rendered. To do this, select **Timeline > Render Work Area**. [**5.1**: Make sure that the entire *Timeline* has been selected with the purplish-blue bar at the top of the *Timeline* — only video inside this area will be rendered. Then move to the *Timeline* and select **Project > Render Selection**.]

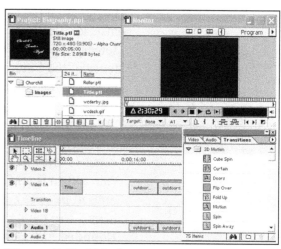

Figure 5.42: Title Insert

 **Figure 5.17:** Play Button

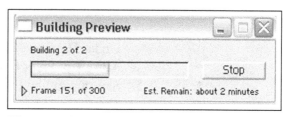

Figure 5.43: Rendering

Adding Rolling Text

1. Start the story of Churchill and Fleming as text rolling up the screen. To do this, begin by selecting **File > New > Title** (F9).

2. After the *Title* window appears, select the **Rolling Text** button on the left side of the *Title* window.

   Click and drag the mouse from the top-left corner to the bottom-right corner of the *Title-Safe* area and let go. A scrolling text box should appear.

Figure 5.44: Roll Tool

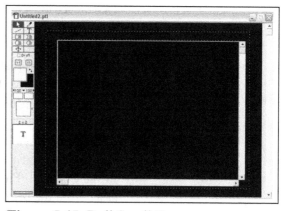

Figure 5.45: Roll Scroll Bar

3. To get the text to roll from the bottom to the top of the screen, click the **Enter** key on the keyboard so the text begins from the bottom instead of halfway up the screen. Type the first sentence of the Churchill/Fleming story from the beginning of this chapter: "While vacationing in Scotland, a young British boy wanders away from his parents and ends up finding himself in quite a predicament." Use the **Arial Rounded MT Bold** font, size **36** point. Use the **Enter** key to start a new line before reaching the edge of the scrolling text bar.

Figure 5.46: Roll Title

4. Next, *right* click inside the *Title* window and select **Rolling Title Options**. Under *Direction*, choose **Move Up**. Press **OK**.

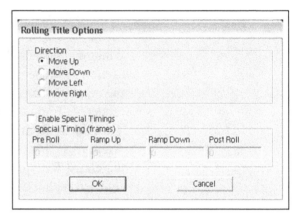

Figure 5.47: Rolling Title Options

5. Save the rolling title by selecting **File > Save As**. Choose the *Churchill's Guardian Angel* folder and name it *Roll* and press **Save**. After saving the title, it should automatically appear in the Bin, ready to be inserted into the *Timeline*. Close the *Title* box and render the rolling title. When rendering is finished, press the **Play** button in the *Monitor* window to view the new title.

Adding Sound

1. Adding a sound file to the video project is much like adding an image file. Use an audio capture utility to narrate the Churchill/Fleming story. If one is not available, use Sound Recorder, found in **Programs > Accessories > Entertainment > Sound Recorder** on most Windows Operating Systems. It should be noted that this capture program only allows for 60-second recordings. Also, it saves recordings as .wav files. Click the **Record** button and read all but the first sentence of the Churchill/Fleming story from the beginning of this chapter. Save this file as *Struggling to end* in the *Churchill's Guardian Angel*

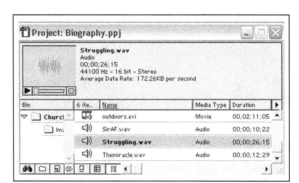

Figure 5.48: Sound File

folder. This should take anywhere from 54 to 58 seconds to read. If read too slowly, the 60-second limit will be exceeded and the piece will need to be read again. If desired, several shorter clips may be read and added individually to the *Timeline*. To add the sound clip to the video, begin by importing the file into the project. Select **File > Import > File (Ctrl + I** or **F3)**, locate the sound, and press **Open**. The sound is now located in the project Bin.

2. Click on the icon next to the sound file's name and drag it to begin around the 16-second mark in the *Audio 2* track on the *Timeline*. This sound file will begin at the same time the outdoors video file begins.

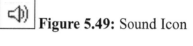 **Figure 5.49:** Sound Icon

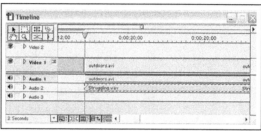

3. To adjust the volume level of the sound file, click on the triangle to the left of the *Audio 1* track. The triangle turns so it is facing down and the audio track opens showing the waveforms of the sound file.

Figure 5.50: Sound Insert

Figure 5.51: Triangle

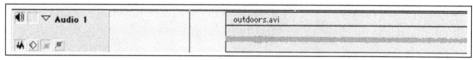

Figure 5.52: Audio Wave

4. To have narration of the Churchill/Fleming story accompanying the video, lower the volume on the audio that was inserted with the video file located on the *Audio 1* track. [**6.0**: Select the **Display Volume Rubberbands** icon (the third icon from the left) and click on the beginning point of the red line located in the middle of the sound file.]

Press and drag the red line down to the bottom of **Figure 5.53:** Audio Band the track. Go to the end of the track and repeat. If the *Audio 1* track volume is not low enough so that the narration sound file on the *Audio 2* track can be heard, raise the red rubber bands in the *Audio 2* track or lower the *Audio 1* track rubber bands even more. [**5.1**: Select the *Audio 1* track. From the toolbar, select **Clip > Audio > Gain**. The *Level Control Gain* dialog box will open. To make the audio level lower, set the percentage below 100%. To make the audio level higher, set the percentage above 100%. Work with the gain percentage until satisfied with the audio level and then click **OK**.]

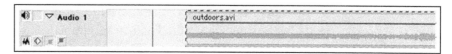

Figure 5.54: Audio Low

5. With the sound clip added, the other clips can be positioned to match more closely with the narrative. A look at the completed *Timeline* view at the beginning of this chapter to see how the segments are placed. Roughly, in order, the *Title* on *Video 1A* lasted five seconds, *Roll* on *Video 1B* lasted 10 seconds, and then the two segments of the outdoors video and audio clip begin on *Video 1A* and *Audio 1* lasted a total of 22 seconds. The narrative (*Struggling ...*) on *Audio 2* begins simultaneously with the *Video 1A* and *Audio 1* tracks. It lasts for 58 seconds. Immediately after the *Video 1A* track ends, digital images start playing on the *Video 2* track. The key is to aim to get the images to play a few seconds before they are mentioned in the narrative or immediately as they are mentioned. For example, when the narrative says, "Winston Churchill became very ill ..." his image should immediately be timed to appear or should appear a few seconds before the narrative. The eight digital picture clips (one used twice) last roughly 4, 4, 7, 3, 3, 5, 6, and 4 seconds, respectively. The image clips are all imported to last four seconds. That works well for the first two clips and last clip. However, the five clips in the middle need to be resized. To do this, choose the **Selection** tool on the *Timeline* window. Then move to the edges between the clips and notice that the cursor turns into what looks like a red "E" with a black arrow in the middle. [**5.1**: The cursor turns into a red "I" with an arrow running through its middle.] The arrow points in which direction(s) the clip may be resized, indicating that the clip can be squished or lengthened, depending on which direction it is pressed or dragged. While resizing clips, scrub the *Timeline* and play the segments several times until segment locations and lengths match the narrative.

Adding Video Transitions

1. **6.0**: To give this digital biography an "aged" look, apply a video transition by selecting **Window > Show Transitions**. Click on the **Video** tab and then select the triangle next to *Image Control* to open it. Select **Black & White** and drag it onto the first video clip in the *Video 1* track. To view the new video footage with the black and white transition, select **Timeline > Render Work Area**. Push the **Play** button in the *Monitor* window to view the video. Repeat this process for each video clip in the *Video 1* track. [**5.1**: To achieve the "aged" look described previously, make sure that the appropriate layer is selected using the **Range Select** tool. Once the layer is selected, choose **Clip > Filters** to open the *Filters* dialog box. Select **Black & White** and click the **Add** button. The **Black & White** option will now appear in the current options section of the *Filters* box. Click **OK** to close the *Filters* dialog box and cause the filter to be applied.]

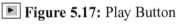 **Figure 5.17:** Play Button

Figure 5.55: Black & White

2. **6.0**: When telling a story with a video, try adding a fun **Page Peel** transition between the title and the rolling title that introduces the story by selecting **Window > Show Transitions**. Click on the tab labeled **Transitions** and then the triangle next to **Page Peel**. [**5.1**: Move the rolling title clip, titled *Roll*, to the *Video 1B* layer. Also make sure that the rolling title overlaps with the *Title* clip located before it in the *Video 1A* layer (this is important because both layers will be visible during the transition). Now, to insert the *Page Peel* transition, select **Window > Show Transitions**. Now scroll through the list of transitions and select the one titled **Page Peel**.]

3. **6.0**: Drag and drop the *Page Peel* transition in between the title and rolling title on the *Video 1* track. To change the duration of any transition, *right* click and select **Duration**. Change the seconds and press **OK**. [**5.1**: Drag and drop the *Page Peel* transition into the *Transition* layer and make sure that the transition fits within the overlap between the title and rolling title. With the transition inserted, *right* click on the transition and choose the **Transition Settings**. A box titled *Page Peel Settings* should appear. Inside of this box, make sure that the arrow next to the transition preview is pointing down (the arrow should be pointing down since the transition is moving from a higher layer in the *Timeline* to a lower layer) and click **OK**. (Note: If there is a video layer overlap outside of a transition, the higher layer will be the one visible in the rendered video.)]

Figure 5.56: Page Peel

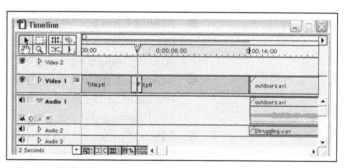

Figure 5.57: Page Insert

Exporting Video

1. There are many formats to choose from when exporting a video in Premiere. One of the most popular is to export the digital biography to videotape for presentation. To do this, first render the entire video before beginning the export process by selecting **Timeline > Render Work Area**.

2. Connect your video camera, with a blank tape inside, to the computer and select **File > Export Timeline > Export to Tape**. [**5.1**: **File > Export > Print to Video**.]

Adaptations and Extensions

Other Ideas to Explore

- To enhance the appearance of the overall presentation, try panning the still images inserted in the video. To do this, *right* click on the image in the *Timeline*; then select **Video Options > Motion**. [**5.1**: **Video > Motion**.] Experiment with the image clip in the top right window of the *Motion Settings* screen. For example, zoom in or out, create a path for the image, or distort the image's appearance.

- Improve the overall quality of the video by making sure the video and audio tracks are synchronized. Consider moving still images to match with related words in the audio so they compliment each other. Also, be sensitive to the end of the movie clip. Do the audio and video tracks end abruptly or fade? Perhaps a rolling credits screen is appropriate or a simple screen that states, "Truth or Fiction? You make the Call!"

- Try out some of the video and audio transitions included in Premiere for interesting effects.

- Turn this digital story into a news feature in which the question of whether the story is fact or fiction is covered in detail. Both the pros and cons can be presented and debated, in short video segments by student experts, before the audience is asked to decide for themselves. See the final bullet in the "Resources" section for more information on the fact or fiction debate.

Curriculum Connections

- **Media Literacy**. Rework the aforementioned news feature story to introduce the evaluation of print-based and online resources for veracity and integrity. Also introduce the concept of urban myths.

- **Science**. Create a similar story on Alexander Fleming's alert observation of the mold in his Petri dishes. Most scientists just discarded those results, but Dr. Fleming did not.

- **Math**. Stories revolving around the Pythagorean Theorem, secrets of the pyramids, or physics problems that can be visualized can be developed in this digital story format.

- **Physical Education**. Find photos of individuals who participate in unhealthy habits like drugs, poor diets, sedentary lifestyle, and little exercise, and show how these people change over time. Visually contrast those photos with photos of individuals with healthy habits.

- **Music**. Create a biography of Bach with examples of his 10 greatest hits.

- **Art**. Pick two artists that lived during the same period of time in two different areas of the world. Visually portray world and local conditions, personal experiences, and training that correspond with the art produced to get a more holistic view of the development of an artist.

Resources

- Tutorials and expert advice for Adobe Premiere can be found at <http://www.tutorialfind.com/tutorials/adobe/premiere> and <http://www.adobe.com/products/tips/premiere.html>.
- Download the *Cookbook and Travelling Companion* from the Center for Digital Storytelling. This free 100-page book is a fantastic resource for taking Premiere to the next level. This is well worth your time! Visit: <http://www.storycenter.org/cookbook.pdf>.
- Consult the Adobe Premiere manual for more information on its advanced features. Also, note that a list of Premiere shortcuts may be accessed by selecting **Window > Show Commands**.
- We first heard the fascinating story of Churchill's guardian angel recited on television when Mark Victor Hansen was asked by a talk show host in Seattle to recite one of his favorite stories from the *Chicken Soup for the Soul* series. The story is titled "Thanks ... Again" and is in the 1996 book *A Cup of Chicken Soup for the Soul* he co-wrote with Jack Canfield and Barry Spilchuk. The version of the story used in this chapter was compiled from the Chicken Soup version and the two URLs that follow. After checking out the Internet sites below, new questions arise. Did Alexander Fleming save Churchill twice or even once? Is the story an urban myth or not? Check out both URLs and then decide for yourself: <http://www.truthorfiction.com/rumors/churchill.htm> and <http://www.winstonchurchill.org/ffleming.htm>.

Glossary

Bins: Containers that include media materials that have been added to the project. They appear on the left side of the project window.

Capture: Importing video material to your computer.

Clips: Individual video or audio segments.

Opacity: A transparent-like effect that allows a clip to fade in or out.

Rubberbands: Red bands on the audio timeline that allows for precise adjustment of the volume level.

Superimpose: Placing clips on top of each other. There are up to 97 superimposed tracks.

Timeline: A window at the bottom of the Premiere screen that includes multiple tracks.

Chapter 6

Vocabulary Cartoons in Flash

Introduction

Make vocabulary come to life with cartoon animations in Macromedia Flash. Flash is a Web-authoring program that allows users to create fast-loading visual content and animations for the Internet.

Arguably, the most important facet of creating cartoon animations is the ability to draw. It is difficult to master the art of animation until one is able to create or obtain the graphics needed for animation. For this tutorial, draw your own pictures or scan in and use pictures provided at the end of the chapter in the "Images for Animation" section.

In this project, a Flash animation, that teaches the meaning of the word "olfactory" and uses the keyword strategy, will be built (Levin, p.235). The keyword method of vocabulary acquisition uses images to create a visual link between the "keyword" and the definition of the vocabulary word. Use a simple three-step process to choose a keyword and remember that olfactory means "sense of smell."

1. Choose a word that you are familiar with, that sounds similar to "olfactory," and that is easy to draw. How about "oil factory?" Generally, nouns are much easier to draw than verbs. An oil factory is also something that most people are familiar with. Oil factory will be used as the keyword.
2. Visually link "oil factory" to the definition "sense of smell" with a picture or an animation. The animation in this example will depict someone being bothered by a terrible smell coming from the oil factory smokestacks.
3. Later, remember that olfactory means "sense of smell" by recalling the visual link between the keyword and the target definition. This is known as a visual mnemonic.

Materials Needed

- Macromedia Flash MX or 5.0
- Photoshop Elements or equivalent photo-editing program
- Scanner
- Digital images (see relevant sections of Chapter 1 and Appendix B)

A Look at the Completed Project

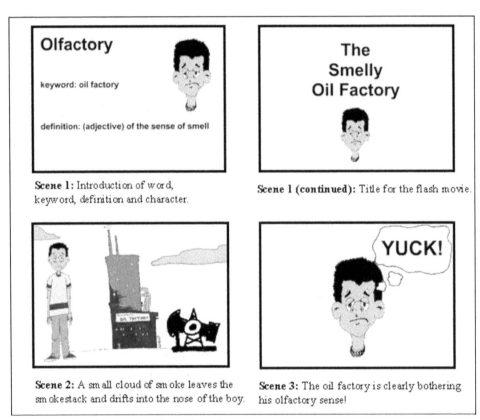

Figure 6.1: Oil Factory Storyboard

Getting Started with a Storyboard

Figure 6.2: Storyboard Drawing

Building the Project

1. Create a new folder on the Desktop to store files for the animation. *Right* click on the Desktop and select **New > Folder** and type "olfactory" to name the folder and press **Enter**.

2. Prepare the graphics by scanning the images from the "Images for Animation" section at the end of this chapter. Follow directions in Appendix B for information on using Photoshop Elements to color and work with images from the scanner. The images should all be saved with transparent backgrounds and given the following names: *boy, boy's face, cloud 1, cloud 2, oil factory, pump up, pump down, smell,* and *thought bubble*. Save these images to the *olfactory* folder on the Desktop.

3. Search the Internet for a sound clip appropriate for the pump (refer to the "Digital Sounds" section in Chapter 1 for more information).

4. Save the audio file to the *olfactory* folder (located on the Desktop).

5. Open Macromedia Flash. Save and name the new file by selecting **File > Save As**; title it *Olfactory*. Be sure to save the file to the *olfactory* folder on the Desktop.

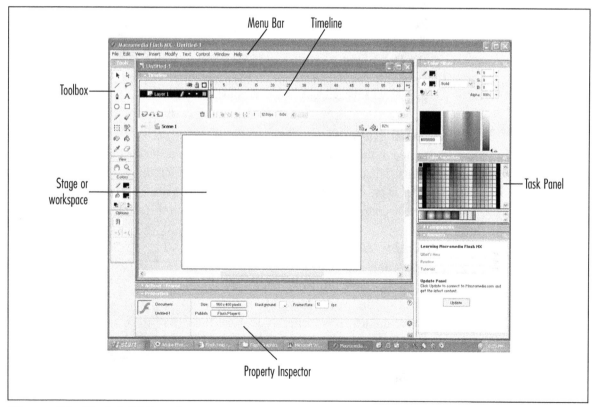

Figure 6.3: Flash MX Interface

Macromedia Flash screen shots reprinted with permission from Macromedia, Inc. Macromedia is a registered trademark of Macromedia, Inc. in the United States and other countries.

6. Turn on *Grid* view by selecting **View > Grid > Show Grid**.

Importing Items to the Library

The library is where all of the components of the animation are stored during the construction process.

1. Open the library by selecting **Windows > Library**.
2. To import the files that will be used in this animation, select **File > Import to Library**. [**5.0**: **File > Import**.] In the *Import to Library* dialog box, navigate to the *olfactory* folder on the Desktop and select the image files that were prepared in the photo-editing program.
3. To select more than one image, hold down the **Ctrl** key while selecting each image. To select all images in a folder, press **Ctrl + A**. Once the image files have been selected, press the **Open** button; this will cause the files to appear in the library. [**5.0**: The files that were imported will appear in the library and the workspace. To remove the images from the workspace, press the **Delete** key.]
4. Save the animation by selecting **File > Save**.

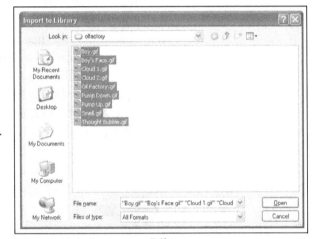

Figure 6.4: Import to Library

Working with Layers

Layers are located in the *Timeline* and can be likened to a stack of transparent sheets stacked on top each other. The order of the layers determines which images appear in the foreground or background. Layers enable the user to divide graphics into separate parts. For example, one image may be changed, while others remain static on different layers.

Renaming Layers

1. Move the cursor to the *Timeline* (located directly above the workspace) and double click on the words **Layer 1**.
2. Once the text has turned blue, type the title "Olfactory" and press *Enter*.

Inserting Layers

1. Select **Insert > Layer** or click on the **Insert Layer** button located at the bottom of the *Timeline*.
2. A new layer will now be generated; rename this layer *Keyword*.
3. Insert one more layer and title it *Boy's Face*.

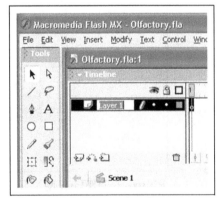

Figure 6.5: Renaming Layers Close Up

 Figure 6.6: Insert Layer Button

Moving Layers

1. The layers should be in the following order from top to bottom: *Olfactory*, *Keyword*, and *Boy's Face*. If the layers are not in the proper order, reorganize them.
2. Select the layer that is not in its proper position and drag and drop the layer to its correct position in the *Timeline*.
3. Repeat these steps if necessary to place the layers in the proper order.
4. To navigate between layers, click once on the layer's title area to select the entire layer or select a frame from the layer's *Timeline*.

Adding and Modifying Text

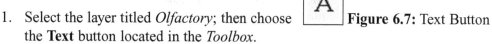

1. Select the layer titled *Olfactory*; then choose the **Text** button located in the *Toolbox*. **Figure 6.7:** Text Button
2. Move the cursor to the workspace, choose a space to insert the text box and click on it once and type the word "Olfactory." Do not worry about the placement of the text on the screen; it will be moved and modified later in the directions.
3. Move to the *Timeline* and click once on the layer titled *Keyword*.
4. With the **Text** button still selected, return to the workspace and click on it once. Insert the text "keyword: oil factory." Press the **Enter** key four times and type "definition: (adjective) of the sense of smell."

Editing Text Properties

1. With the **Text** button still selected, click on the *Olfactory* layer in the *Timeline*.
2. Click once on the word "Olfactory" in the workspace; this should cause a text box to appear around the word.
3. Highlight the word "Olfactory" by holding down the mouse and dragging it across the text; then release the mouse key.
4. Move to the *Property Inspector* (located at the bottom of the screen). If the *Inspector* is minimized, click once on the small triangle button to the left of the word "Properties" to restore to full size. [**5.0**: Since this version of Flash is without a *Property Inspector*, move to the toolbar at the top of the screen and select **Text > Character** to open the *Character* dialog box.]
5. With the text still highlighted, the *Property Inspector* should be in text mode. The *Inspector* is context sensitive. If text is selected, the contents of the *Inspector* change, providing options to modify the text. If a graphic image is selected, it changes to provide options for modifying graphics.

Figure 6.8: Text Property Inspector

6. Change the font type to **Arial** and the font size to **48** point. Also select a **Black** color as well as **Bold** and **Left Justified** options. [**5.0**: The *Character* dialog box contains options for all font changes, except left justify. To do this, click on the **Paragraph** tab located at the top of the *Character* dialog box (if the tab is not there, move to the *Toolbox* and select **Text > Paragraph**) and select the **Left Justified** button.]
7. Move to the *Timeline* and switch to the *Keyword* layer.
8. Highlight the text and change the font properties to **Arial**, **24** point, **Black**, and **Left Justified**.

Moving Text

1. Move the cursor to the *Toolbox* and select the black **Arrow** tool.

 Figure 6.9: Arrow Tool

2. In the *Timeline*, select the *Olfactory* layer.
   A blue box should appear around the text. If not, click once on the word "Olfactory" (located in the workspace).
3. Drag the text box to upper-left-hand corner of the workspace, specifically one gridline from the top and one gridline from the left. Then release the mouse key.
4. Select the *Keyword* layer from the *Timeline*.
5. Move the text in this layer to the fourth gridline below the word "Olfactory" and one gridline from the left. (Note: Pressing the **arrow keys** on the keyboard can also move selected text and other objects.)
6. Once completed save the animation.

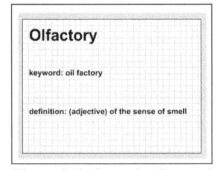

Figure 6.10: Scene 1 — Layout 1

Converting Text to a Symbol

Symbols are elements (graphics, buttons, sound files, video clips, or fonts) that can be reused in a Flash file and are stored in the library. They reduce the size of the file — no matter how many times a symbol is used in a file, Flash only stores it once.

1. Select the *Olfactory* layer in the *Timeline* by clicking once on the word "Olfactory."
2. Select **Insert > Convert to Symbol**.
3. Name the symbol *Olfactory* and make the behavior a **Graphic**. With these preferences chosen, select **OK**.

Figure 6.11: Convert to Symbol

4. Select the *Keyword* layer in the *Timeline* and convert the text in this layer to a symbol.
5. Name the file *Keyword* and select **Graphic** for the behavior.

Adding and Modifying Images

1. Move to the *Timeline* and select the layer named *Boy's Face*.
2. Move the cursor to the library. If the library is not present, press **F11** on the keyboard. Use the scroll bar on the right side of the library to find *Boy's Face* and select it. An image of the boy's face will appear in the library.
3. Drag the image of the boy's face from the library to the workspace and release it.

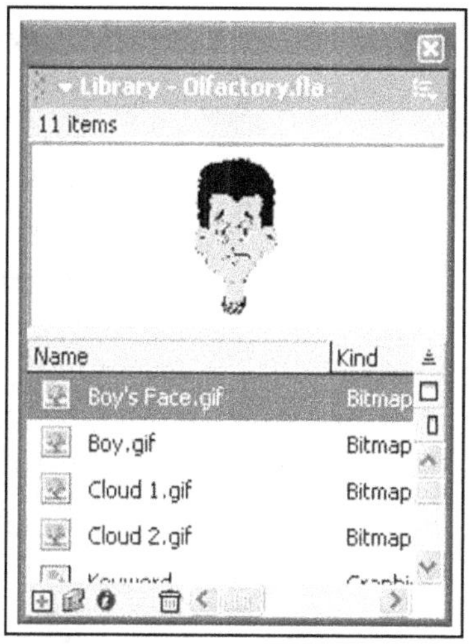

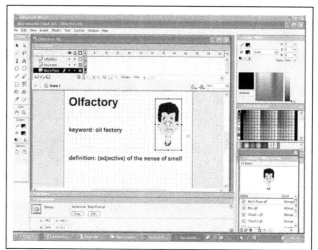

Figure 6.12: Boy's Face in the Library

Scaling Images

1. *Right* click on the image of the boy's face and select the **Scale** option. This will cause small squares to appear around the perimeter of the image.
2. Hold down the **Ctrl** key while pressing down on one of the corner squares and move the cursor outward to make the image larger or inward to make the image smaller as needed. Make the boy's face an appropriate size on the screen. Release the mouse key and then click anywhere outside of the image.

Moving Images

1. Select the black **Arrow** tool and click once on the image of the boy's face, located in the workspace. A box will appear around the image.
2. Press down inside the box. While holding down the mouse, drag the box to the right of the text; then release the mouse key.
3. Convert the image to a symbol by clicking once on the image of the boy's face and select **Insert > Convert to Symbol**.
4. Name the symbol *Boy's Face* and make the behavior a **Graphic** and press **OK**.

Figure 6.13: Scene 1 —Layout 2

Working with the Timeline: Creating a Fading Text Effect

Note: The *Timeline* represents the passage of time within the animation; it is organized into a series of frames that are played at a specified rate.

Inserting Keyframes
A keyframe is a special frame where a change occurs in an animation (elements may be rotated, resized, added, removed, re-colored, faded, and so on).

1. Move to the *Olfactory* layer in the *Timeline* and click on Frame 10.
2. Select **Insert > Keyframe (F6)**.

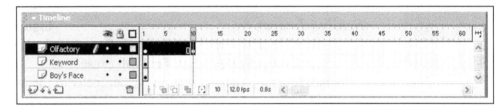

Figure 6.14: Timeline with First Keyframe

3. Repeat this process for the *Keyword* and *Boy's Face* layers.

Creating a Motion Tween
Tween is short for the word "between." Tweening fills in the missing images between two keyframes to create the illusion of motion or change. Tweening minimizes the amount of work needed to create an animation.

1. Return to the *Olfactory* layer in the *Timeline*. The frames in this layer will now appear black.
2. Select **Insert > Create Motion Tween**.

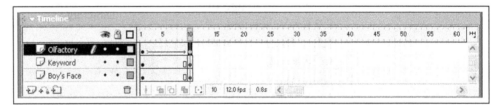

Figure 6.15: Timeline with Motion Tween

3. Repeat this process for the *Keyword* and *Boy's Face* layers. Notice when the frames are de-selected, they will now appear light purple and will contain a directional arrow.
4. Save the animation.

Fading Symbols

Fade In

1. **MX**: Select the first frame of the *Olfactory* layer. With the **Arrow** tool selected in the *Toolbox*, click once on the *Olfactory* symbol in the workspace. The *Property Inspector* should now be in graphic mode. [**5.0**: Since this version of Flash does not have a *Property Inspector*, move to the menu at the top of the screen and select **Windows > Panels > Effect** to open the *Effect* dialog box.]
2. The *Color* window [**5.0**: *Effect* window] will contain a single drop-down box with the word "None" in it. Press the down arrow key to the right of this box.
3. Choose the **Alpha** option. Alpha refers to the level of transparency applied to an object. A new dialog box will appear to the right of it. Set the alpha percentage to **zero**. When the percentage is changed, the symbol should disappear.

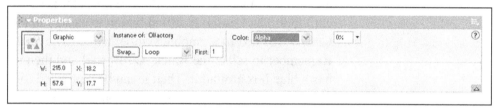

Figure 6.16: Graphic Property Inspector

4. Repeat this process for the *Keyword* and *Boy's Face* layers.

Fade Out

1. Move to the *Olfactory* layer in the *Timeline* and click on Frame 110 by moving the slider bar at the bottom of the *Timeline*.
2. Create a new keyframe in this location by selecting **Insert > Keyframe (F6)** and repeat this for the *Keyword* and *Boy's Face* layers.
3. Select the Frame 120 in the *Olfactory* layer and create a keyframe there. Repeat for the *Keyword* and *Boy's Face* layers.
4. Return to the keyframe 120 in the *Olfactory* layer and select it.
5. Move to the workspace [**5.0**: *Effect* dialog box] and select the word "Olfactory" (a text symbol).
6. In the *Property Inspector* [**5.0**: *Effect* dialog box], select the *Color* window by clicking on the down arrow and choose the **Alpha** option. A new box will appear; change its alpha percentage to **zero**. The symbol will disappear. (Tip: There is so much white space in the *Keyword* text box that it seems to help if users click directly on the text in order for the *Property Inspector* to change to the graphic mode.)
7. Repeat this process for the *Keyword* and *Boy's Face* layers.

Previewing the Animation

1. Select the first frame in the *Timeline* within any of the layers and press the **Enter** key to play the animation.
2. During the course of the animation, the text and the image will fade in, will stay on the screen for a few moments, and will then fade out.
3. Save the animation.

Constructing the Title Information

1. Insert a new layer and give it the name *Title*.
2. Move the *Title* layer below the *Boy's Face* layer in the *Timeline*.
3. Select Frame 125 in the *Title* layer and insert a keyframe.
4. Select the **Text** tool and in the workspace type the animation title "The" and press **Enter**; type "Smelly" and press **Enter**; type "Oil Factory."
5. Highlight the text and set the text properties as **Arial**, **48** point, **Black**, **Bold**, and **Center Justified**. (Note: Be sure the color is set to black, not to transparent.) [**5.0**: The **Center Justified** button is located in the *Paragraph* dialog box.]
6. Convert the text to a graphic symbol named *The Smelly Oil Factory*. Remember to select the **Black Arrow** tool and then select the text so that it has a blue box around it. Then it can be converted to a symbol (shortcut: **F8**).
7. With the **Arrow** tool selected, click once on the new symbol and drag it to the second grid from the top of the workspace and center the symbol on the horizontal axis.
8. In the *Boy's Face* layer in the *Timeline*, select Frame 125 and insert a new keyframe.
9. Turn the alpha off to see the symbol. Do this by selecting the invisible box containing the boy's face. The *Property Inspector* will change into graphic mode. [**5.0**: Move to the *Effect* dialog box.]
10. Make sure **Alpha** is selected in the *Color* window and change the alpha to **100%**.
11. Scale the symbol of the *Boy's Face* and center it under the title.
12. Turn the alpha in the *Boy's Face* layer back to **0%**.
13. Move to the *Title* layer and select Frame 135 and insert a new keyframe.
14. Select all of the frames in this layer by clicking on any other layer in the *Timeline* and then clicking once on the word "Title" in the *Title* layer. The selected frames will appear black.
15. **Insert > Create Motion Tween**.

Figure 6.17: Scene 1 — Layout 3

16. Move to *Title* layer, Frame 125, and create an alpha fade in by setting the color to **Alpha 0%**.
17. Move to the *Boy's Face* layer, Frame 135.
18. Insert a new keyframe and turn the alpha to **None** in the *Color* window.
19. Move to *Boy's Face* layer, Frame 175, and insert a new keyframe.
20. Move to the *Title* layer, Frame 175, and insert a new keyframe.
21. Move to Frame 185 and insert a new keyframe in both the *Title* and *Boy's Face* layers.
22. In both the *Title* and *Boy's Face* layers, create an alpha fade out by setting **Alpha** to **0%**.
23. Save the file and preview the animation.

Working with Scenes

Just as a theatrical play is divided into several scenes, so are Flash movies. A scene is a subdivision in the *Timeline* that allows for the organization and simplification of layers. Everything done thus far has been created in Scene 1. Now to create Scene 2:

1. Select **Insert > Scene**. The layers in the first scene will disappear.

Moving Between Scenes
1. **MX**: The *Scene Bar* is located between the workspace and the *Timeline*. [**5.0**: The *Scene Bar* is located directly above the *Timeline*.]

Figure 6.18: Scene Bar

2. The left side of this bar will indicate that Scene 2 is currently selected. Move the mouse to the right side of the bar and select the **Clipboard** button.
3. Click on the **Clipboard** button and select Scene 1.
4. The *Scene Bar* will indicate that Scene 1 is currently being viewed. Return to Scene 2 via the **Clipboard** button. **Figure 6.19:** Clipboard Icon

Working with Animated Symbols

Creating Animated Symbols
1. Select **Insert > New Symbol**.
2. Title the symbol *Pump*.
3. Set the behavior of the animation as a movie clip and press **OK**. The *Timeline* should be blank.
4. Name the existing layer *Pump Up*.

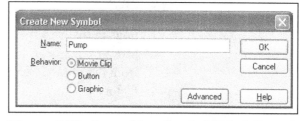

Figure 6.20: Create New Symbol Titled "Pump"

5. Insert another layer and name it *Pump Down*.
6. Insert the image of the *Pump Up* in the *Pump Up* layer by dragging it from the library (shortcut: **F11**) to the screen.
7. Insert the image of the *Pump Down* in the *Pump Down* layer.
8. Scale the images to appropriate matching sizes.
9. Move to the *Pump Up* layer, Frame 7, and insert a new keyframe.
10. Move to the *Pump Down* layer, Frame 1, and click on that keyframe.
11. Hold down on the mouse key and drag the keyframe to Frame 8. Move to Frame 14 and insert a new keyframe.
12. Move to the *Scene Bar* and click on Scene 2. The Scene 2 *Timeline* will appear.
13. Title the existing layer *Oil Factory* and insert the image of the oil factory from the library.

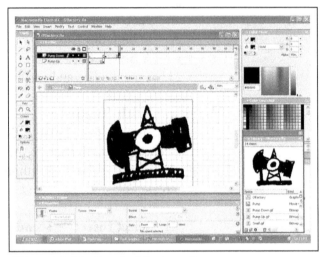

Figure 6.21: Symbol Layout 2

14. Scale the image to fit the workspace and convert the image to a graphic symbol called *Oil Factory*.

Inserting Animated Symbols

1. Insert a new layer (place it above the *Olfactory* layer) and name the layer *Pump*.
2. Insert the animated symbol called *Pump* from the library, placing the image on the right side of the oil factory.
3. Scale the symbol as necessary.

Adding Three New Layers

1. Insert three new layers in the *Timeline*. Title the first layer *Boy*, the second layer *Clouds*, and the third layer *Smell*.
2. Move to the *Boy* layer in the *Timeline* and insert the image of the boy from the library and scale the image. Place it to the left of the oil factory.
3. Move to the *Clouds* layer in the *Timeline* and insert the two images of the clouds from the library. Scale the images and place them in appropriate positions in the workspace.
4. Move to the *Smell* layer in the *Timeline* and insert the image of the smell from the library. Scale the image and place it above the chimney of the oil factory.

5. Convert the images in the three new layers to graphic symbols and title them by name (*Clouds*, *Smell*, and *Boy*).
6. Move to Frame 10 in the *Timeline* and insert a new keyframe in each of the layers.
7. Convert the frames in each layer into a motion tween.
8. Move back to the first frame in the *Timeline*

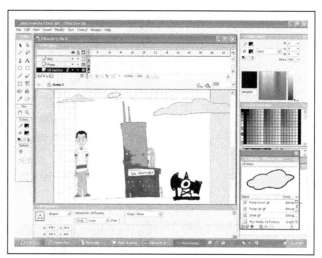

Figure 6.22: Scene 2 — Layout 1

and create an Alpha fade in for each of the layers. (Set the first frame in each layer to the color **Alpha** at **0%**.)

Creating a Motion Tween

1. Move to Frame 25 in the *Timeline* and insert a new keyframe in the *Smell*, *Boy*, and *Oil Factory* layers.
2. Move to the Frame 25 in the *Smell* layer and click on the *Smell* symbol.
3. Holding down on the mouse key, drag the symbol over the boy's face.
4. Rescale the symbol so that it is noticeable.

Creating a Motion Guide

1. Select the *Smell* layer in the *Timeline* and then choose **Insert > Motion Guide**. *Guide: Smell* will now appear in the *Timeline*.

Figure 6.23: Timeline with Motion Guide

2. Select the entire *Guide* layer by clicking on the *Guide* title once.
3. In the *Toolbox* (located in the left side of the screen), select the **Pencil** button.

Figure 6.24: Pencil Button

4. Move to the *Options* box below the *Toolbox* and make sure that the *Pencil* mode is set as smooth.
5. Draw a curved line between the point where the symbol will begin in Frame 10 and the point where the symbol will end in Frame 25.

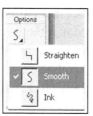

Figure 6.25: Pencil Options

6. **MX**: Select the entire *Smell* layer. The *Property Inspector* should now be in **Frame** mode. [**5.0**: Move to the *Toolbar* at the top of the screen and select **Windows > Panels > Frame** to open the *Frame* dialog box.]

7. In the *Frame* dialog box, make sure the **Sync** and **Snap** check boxes are selected.

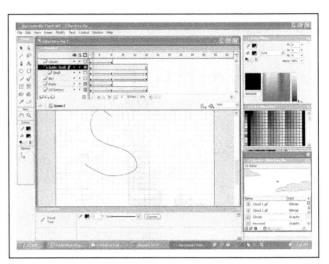

Figure 6.26: Scene 2 — Layout 3

Figure 6.27: Frame Property Inspector

8. In the *Timeline*, move to Frame 35 in the *Smell* layer and create a keyframe.
9. Create a fade out for this layer by setting the **Alpha** to **0%** on this frame.
10. Preview and save the animation.

Adding the Thought Bubble

1. Insert a new layer, above the *Guide: Smell* layer, and title the new layer *Thought Bubble*.
2. Move to Frame 35 in the *Timeline* and insert a keyframe. In the new keyframe, insert the image of the thought bubble from the library.
3. Move to the *Boy* layer and insert a keyframe in the Frame 35.
4. Return to the *Thought Bubble* layer and scale the image, placing it next to the boy's head.
5. Create another layer. Make sure this layer is above the *Thought Bubble* layer and title the new layer *Text*.
6. Move to Frame 35 and insert a keyframe.
7. In the workspace, insert the text "The smelly" and press **Enter**; type "oil factory bothers" and press **Enter**; type "my olfactory sense."
8. Set the text properties as **Arial**, **Black**, **Bold**, and **Center Justified**.
9. Match the font size to the thought bubble.
10. Convert the objects in the two new layers into appropriately named graphic symbols.
11. Move to Frame 45 in the *Timeline* and insert a new keyframe in the two new layers.
12. Create a motion tween for both layers.

13. Convert the motion tween in each layer into a fade in by setting the color as **Alpha 0%** on Frame 35.
14. Move to Frame 85 and insert a new keyframe for the *Text*, *Thought Bubble*, *Clouds*, *Boy*, *Pump*, and *Oil Factory* layers.
15. Move to Frame 95 in the *Timeline* and insert a new keyframe for each of the layers listed in the previous step. Then create a fade out for each of the layers.
16. Save the animation.

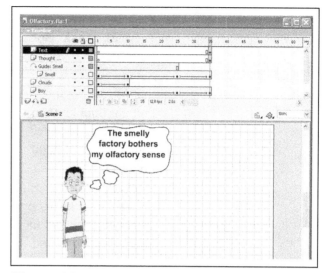

Figure 6.28: Scene 2 — Layout 4

Inserting Audio

1. In the *Timeline*, insert a new layer named *Audio*. Place this layer above the *Text* layer.
2. Import the audio clip to the library by selecting **File > Import to Library**.
3. With the *Audio* layer selected, drag the audio clip to the workspace.
4. Move to Frame 1 in the *Audio* layer.
5. The audio waves will appear in the *Timeline*; move to the end of the waves and press the **F6** key to create a new keyframe.
6. Stay in the new keyframe and drag a new copy of the audio file into the layer.
7. Repeat this as often as needed to reach the end of the animation.

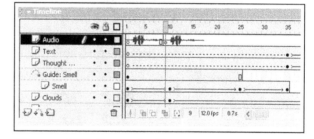

Figure 6.29: Pump Audio

Adding Scene Three

1. Insert a new scene (*Scene 3*).
2. Rename the existing layer *Boy's Face*.
3. Create two more layers and title the layers *Thought Bubble* and *Text*.
4. Place the graphic images of the boy's face and the thought bubble from the library into the corresponding layers.
5. Move to the *Boy's Face* layer and scale the image to an appropriate size; center the image in the lower half of the screen.
6. Move to the *Thought Bubble* layer and scale the image to an appropriate size; place the image to the right side of the boy's face.
7. Move to the layer titled *Text* and type the word "YUCK!" in the workspace.

8. Set the text properties as **Arial**, **Black**, **Bold**, and **Center Justified**. Set the font to a size that fits within the thought bubble; then move the text to the center of the thought bubble.

9. Convert the image and text from the layers previously mentioned into appropriately named graphic symbols.

Figure 6.30: Scene 3—Layout 1

10. Move to Frame 10 in the *Timeline* and insert a keyframe for each layer.

11. Convert the frames in each layer into a motion tween.

12. Make each of the motion tweens fade in by setting Frame 1 in each layer to **Alpha 0%**.

13. Move to Frame 25 in the *Timeline* and insert a keyframe in all of the layers.

14. Repeat this process and create a keyframe in Frame 35 and in all of the layers.

15. In the final keyframe of each layer, set the **Alpha** to **0%** to create a fade out.

16. Save the animation.

Exporting SWF Files

1. To export the file as an SWF file, select **File > Export Movie**.

2. Title the file "olfactory" and press the **Save** button. The *Export Flash Player Pop-up* dialog box will appear. Click **OK**.

3. Close Macromedia Flash to view the animation.

4. Open the *olfactory* folder (located on the Desktop).

5. Double click the file named *olfactory.swf*. The *Flash Viewer* will open and the olfactory animation will begin to play.

Figure 6.31: Export Movie

Figure 6.32: Export Flash Player

Adaptations and Extensions

Other Ideas to Explore

- Add voice narrations reading the word, definitions, and part of speech in an additional layer in the example.
- Create a button to activate or stop the "olfactory" animation.
- Investigate the different tweening effects in Flash—creating motion paths, changing the size or color of an object, or creating the illusion of motion by inserting sequential pictures in motion in the keyframes.
- Add additional scenes to the olfactory example using the keyword in a sentence such as, "My olfactory sense told me that someone had been smoking in the room." Add a still picture to visually depict the sentence.
- Use Flash MX's new templates by selecting **File > New From Template** and choose **Presentation** to help create great slides.

Curriculum Connection

- **Vocabulary**. Animate difficult vocabulary words for nearly any subject area using the template for the first scene in this tutorial.
- **Upper Elementary — High School**. Use the tutorial to teach students how to use the keyword method to learn vocabulary words.
- **Science**. Animate the most difficult terms or concepts covered throughout the year.
- **Computers**.
  1. Have students script and storyboard keyword animations for difficult concepts or words in other subject areas.
  2. Have students use the fade in and fade out animation effects in other projects.
  3. Compare and contrast the animation effects of MORPH (or any other morphing software package) with the tweening tools in Flash.
- **Art**.
  1. Have students draw still pictures used in the animation.
  2. Experiment with drawing a sequence of pictures needed to animate motion. How many images are necessary to make the motion realistic? Scan the images and prepare them in a photo-editing program; then view and evaluate the animations in Flash.

Resources

- To learn the basics about Flash, check out the **Lessons** included in Flash or take a tour through the **Tutorials**. Select **Help** on the *Menu Bar* to find either option. Look up specific terms or directions by selecting **Using Flash**, which is also located on the **Help** menu.
- Try out Macromedia Flash for free and access Macromedia's online tutorials at <http://www.macromedia.com/software/flash/productinfo/tutorials>.

- To access online Flash tutorials check out Tutorialfind at <http://www.tutorialfind.com/tutorials/macromedia>.
- CNET Builder.com contains tips for customizing your interface, working with new action scripts, improving regular workflow, and utilizing the drawing tools. Visit <http://builder.cnet.com/webbuilding/ 0-7335-8-3993307-1.html?tag+st.con.1.tlpg.7335-8-3993307-1>.
- Want to add video files into Flash to post them on the Web? Try out a program called Flix by Wildform that converts video into a Web-friendly format.
- Improve your ability to draw with Mark Kistler's *Draw Squad*, a great book for upper elementary and beyond.

Glossary

Alpha: Pertains to the amount of transparency applied to an object.

Keyframe: A frame where a change is defined in an animation, or includes frame actions to modify a movie.

Layers: Divisions in the timeline that allow for the separation of objects to create a more accessible environment during the animation process.

Library: Where all of the components of the animation are stored during the construction process.

Property Inspector: A context sensitive area at the bottom of the screen in version MX that contains options for working with and modifying a document.

Scene: A subdivision in the timeline that allows for the organization and simplification of layers.

Symbols: Elements (graphics, buttons, sound files, video clips, or fonts) that can be reused in a Flash file and are stored in the library. Symbols reduce the size of the file—no matter how many times a symbol is used in a file, Flash only stores it once.

Timeline: Represents the passage of time within the animation. It is organized into a series of frames that are played at a specified rate.

Tweening: Is short for the word "between." Tweening fills in the missing images between two keyframes to create the illusion of motion or change. Tweening minimizes the amount of work needed to create animation.

Images for Animation

Figure 6.33: Boy

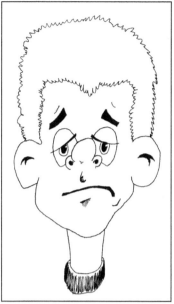

Figure 6.34: Boy's Face

Figure 6.35: Cloud 1

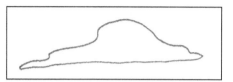

Figure 6.36: Cloud 2

Figure 6.38:
Pump Down

Figure 6.39:
Pump Up

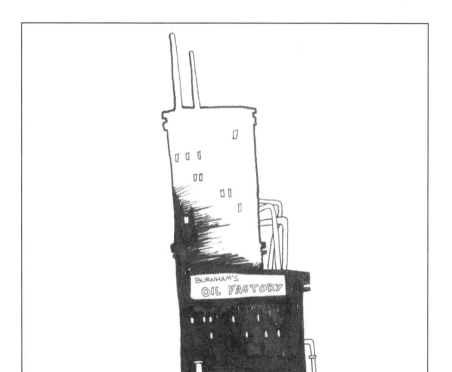

Figure 6.37: Oil Factory

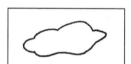

Figure 6.40: Smell

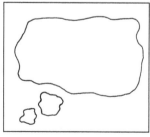

Figure 6.41: Thought
Bubble

Chapter 7

Tips to Better Digital Stories

Take your own digital stories to a new level using the design and presentation tips in this chapter. Find just the right pieces of clip art, pictures, and sounds for your project using the links in the "Online Resources" section. Also learn more about digital storytelling and copyrights. These links were all working as of February 25, 2003. Be aware that links online today may be gone tomorrow.

Design Tips

1. **Find the nugget of the story and build around it!** Focus on the essence of the story. Basically, get to the point. Too often when people start building their stories, they start with concepts that are way too big and too elaborate and that have too many images and sounds. By the time the digital story is created, they wonder why people didn't respond more favorably. For the audience, watching these types of stories can be similar to viewing unedited home movies of a distant relative. Most often, this is not an enjoyable experience.

2. **Backwards Storyboarding.** Storyboard the final scene first. Start with the proverbial punch line and then work backward to the beginning. What should the audience leave with after experiencing this story? How should it end? By storyboarding the final scene first, designers are forced to articulate the objective of the digital story. By knowing where the story will end, the process of storyboarding the rest of the show is generally made easier.

3. **Thematic Designing.** This design principle is about making sure there is harmony among the design elements of the story. The fonts, clip art, music, sound effects, and background colors should all fit the theme of the presentation. For example, even the font used in the opening title of a digital story

can have a positive effect on the viewer. Observe how Hollywood movies often will use a font title that matches the theme for the movie. Even in the old western movies, the titles were created in a style, like the "wrangler font," that matches the western theme. A great place to develop font titles is at <http://www.flamingtext.com>. Be sure to look at the thematic styles available in the headings area. A word of caution is in order: Less is generally more. This refers to the fact that overdoing it in this area can be distracting to the audience and can have a negative effect on the viewers' perceptions of the story. Too many sound effects, too many descriptive fonts, and too many animated gifs running around the screen can be very distracting. In initial design and development of digital stories, it is recommended that new designers err on the side of using less of these types of special effects.

Presentation Tips

1. **Presentation Options.** Some digital stories are just a small part of a presentation and, sometimes, they are the entire presentation. Either way, it might be useful to look at some of the presentation options. Presenting digital stories from a laptop via a projection system is fairly common. Sending an e-mail with shorter stories attached is also becoming commonplace. For example, PowerPoint stories can be sent as a PowerPoint Show (.pps file) complete with timings (**Slide Show > Rehearse Timings**) and should play automatically when opened. Flash stories can be showcased online and are ready to play once someone visits the site. Studio and Premiere stories can be saved to videotape. With the right equipment, PowerPoint files can also be saved to videotape. In the August, 2002, issue of *Presentations Magazine* (p.13), Julie Hill covers two ways to save PowerPoint to video, one of which involves using Adobe Premiere. CDs and DVDs are also excellent ways to save digital stories.

2. **Practice, Practice, Practice.** If presenting the digital story in a live setting, make sure to work out your timing with the technology. Practice it, hone it, tweak it, work with it, and get comfortable with the technology part of the delivery. Timing can be a critical component in digital storytelling. Like telling a good joke, knowing when and how to deliver the punch line is often the key to how funny the joke is perceived. Timing the delivery can be a critical ingredient to the impact the story can have.

   An interesting idea that some have used successfully is to time your delivery with a talking animated character in the story. Vox Proxy <http://www.voxproxy.com> sells these characters that can be easily programmed and timed to interact with a presenter.

3. **Remote Controls.** Some presenters seem as though they are chained to the computer when presenting. Actually they are — tethered to the computer by a little device called the mouse. One way presenters can break free is to use a remote control. Keyspan's <http://www.keyspan.com> Presentation Remote has been given the highest rating possible rating in *Presentations Magazine* (September, 2002).

Online Resources

New technological tools allow teachers to tell powerful multimedia-driven stories. To keep on top of this fast paced and rapidly evolving field, it is advisable to keep abreast of the online resources available. The following digital storytelling links should do the trick.

Corporate Links

A focus on how digital storytelling relates to branding and online marketing.

1. **Fast Company — Storytelling and Work**. Visit <http://www.fastcompany.com/team/hrowstory.html>
2. **Business Week — The Power of Digital Storytelling**: a hot new trend in online marketing. Visit <http://www.businessweek.com/2000/00_20/b3681104.htm> and <http://www.businessweek.com/2000/00_20/b3681103.htm>.

The Future of Digital Storytelling

1. **Hamlet on the Holodeck**, guidebook of the future of storytelling, published by MIT Press. Available at <http://web.mit.edu/jhmurray/www/HOH.html>.
2. **The OZ Project at CMU** is developing the technology and art to create high-quality interactive drama. More specifically, they are attempting to build believable agents in dramatically interesting micro-worlds. Visit <http://www-2.cs.cmu.edu/afs/cs.cmu.edu/project/oz/web/oz.html>.

Current Debates

1. **Digital Storytelling: Is it Art?** A fascinating give-and-take discussion and disagreement regarding the promises of digital media between Dr. Janet H. Murray and Dr. Sven Birkerts. Visit <http://hotwired.lycos.com/synapse/braintennis/97/31/index0a.html>.

Links with More Links ...

1. **The Digital Storytelling Conference & Festival**. Visit <http://www.dstory.com/dsf6/links.html>.
2. **Digital storytelling links from Tech-Head**. Visit <http://tech-head.com/dstory.htm>.
3. **Syllabus for a digital storytelling course at Berkeley**. Visit <http://www-writing.berkeley.edu/digitalstory>.
4. **The Story Place**. Visit <http://www.storycenter.org/storyplace.html>.

Online Media Resources

Image Search Engines

1. <http://images.google.com> Typing in "frogs" returns pictures and clip art of frogs. When looking for clip art, or cartoon style images of frogs, type in "frogs .gif" (without the quotes). When looking for pictures of frogs, type in "frogs .jpg" to narrow the search to .jpg type images. When the results appear, click on the thumbnail of the image considered for use. Then click on the link just below the image that says something like *See full-size image*. Finally, download the image to the computer or click on the **Back** button on the browser to return to Google. This was the only search engine in this list that found results for "princess kissing frog."
2. <http://ditto.com> This search engine was created for searching images only.
3. <http://www.attavista.com> Click on the **Image** tab at the top of the *Search* window. Over 25 million images are cataloged here.
4. <http://ixquick.com> Click the **Pictures** radio button above the *Search* window and type in your search.

Popular Clip Art Sites

1. <http://www.pics4learning.com> (copyright-friendly images for education)
2. <http://www.allseasonclipart.com>
3. <http://www.clipartconnection.com>
4. <http://www.arttoday.com>
5. <http://www.barrysclipart.com>
6. <http://www.animfactory.com> (animations)

Online Sound Resources

1. <http://www.altavista.com> Click on the **Video** tab at the top of the *Search* window. Well over a million sound files are indexed by Altavista.
2. <http://soundzabound.com> This site offers royalty free music library — 3 CDs for $99.

Intellectual Property Rights

Fair-Use Guidelines

1. <http://fairuse.stanford.edu> Fair-Use Guidelines
2. <http://www.utsystem.edu/ogc/intellectualproperty/cprtindx.htm> Crash Course in Copyright
3. <http://www.utsystem.edu/ogc/intellectualproperty/ccmcguid.htm> Fair-Use Guidelines for Educational Multimedia
4. <http://www.benedict.com> This is branded as the copyright Web site. Showcased here are some of the legal battles over visual and audio copyrights.

For example, the producers of *Batman Forever* were sued for including a Los Angeles based sculpture in the movie.

5. *Copyright for Schools: a Practical Guide* by Carol Simpson (2001, Linworth Publishing). Dr. Simpson is an expert in this area and is regularly called upon to present at national conferences on this topic.

Public Domain

1. <http://www.google.com/unclesam> This resource at Google only searches the .gov and .mil sites on the Internet. Type "frogs wav" (without the quotes) to discover copyright free frog sounds.

2. <http://www.surweb.org> Thousands of royalty free images, sounds, and movies are provided at the state of Utah Resources Web site.

3. <http://images.google.com> Images found at this site are unlikely to be found in the public domain, unless the image searches are limited to just government sites. In the Google search box, type in "site:.gov frogs" (without the quotes). This will limit your "frogs" search to just government sites.

Copyright-Friendly

1. <http://www.pics4learning.com> This site contains hundreds of copyright-friendly images for teachers and students. These pictures have been donated by amateur photographers, students, and teachers. Be sure to check out the "100 Most Popular Images" link at the top of the page.

2. <http://www.freefoto.com> The site contains over 30,000 free photographs for private, non-commercial use on the Internet.

Appendix A
Storyboard Templates

The following two storyboards can be copied and used to develop your digital stories. The first storyboard was created in PowerPoint. For directions on how to create it from PowerPoint, see the section in Chapter 1 titled "Getting Started with Storyboards."

The second storyboard is more detailed and is designed for projects using video, audio, and other media.

Figure A.1: Blank PowerPoint Storyboard

Figure A.2: Multimedia Storyboard

Appendix B
Working with Images in Photoshop Elements Version 2.0

Scanning Images from this Book

1. Make a folder on your Desktop and label it "images." This is where you will save all of your images.
2. Open Adobe Photoshop Elements. Select **Connect to Camera or Scanner**. In the *Select Import Source* window, select your scanner using the down arrow and press **OK**.

    If Photoshop Elements is already open, select **File > Import**; then select your scanner from the drop-down menu. Your scanner program will fill the Desktop.
3. Start a new scan. The scanner program should automatically send the scan to Photoshop Elements. If not, save the scanned image to a folder on the Desktop.
4. Try changing the *Output Type* to **Black and White Drawing**. This will convert the picture to a Bitmap image in Photoshop Elements.
5. Change the selection border by moving the border to get rid of extra white space and to reduce the file size.
6. Send the scan.

Working with Scanned Images in Photoshop Elements

The scan should now appear in Photoshop Elements. The Photoshop Elements interface is shown in Figure B.1 on the following page.

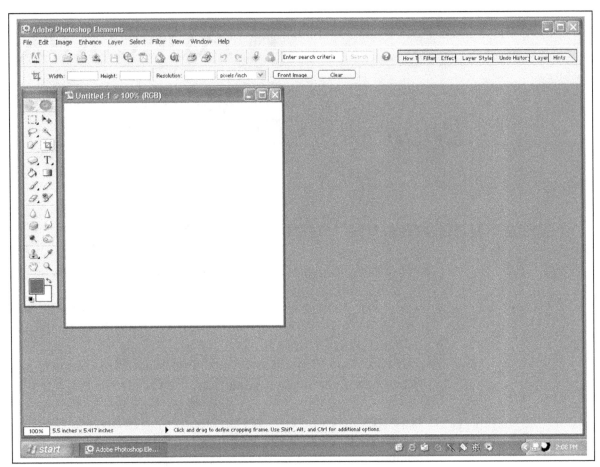

Figure B.1: Photoshop Elements Interface

Adobe® Photoshop Elements® screen shots reprinted with permission from Adobe Systems, Inc. Adobe Photoshop Elements is a registered trademarks of Adobe Systems Incorporated in the United States and other countries.

Enlarge the work area by selecting the **Maximize** button located at the top-right corner of the work screen. A gray border will fill the screen around the image.

 Figure B.2: Maximize Button

Undoing Mistakes

1. To Undo your last command, press **Edit > Step Backward** or **Ctrl + Z**. To redo your last command, select **Edit > Step Forward** or **Ctrl + Y**.
2. Another method is to click on the **Undo History** tab at the top right of the screen. A list of the most recent actions performed in Photoshop Elements will appear in the drop-down menu. Use the scrollbar on the left side to find the command you wish to undo. Click on the command to see what the image looked like up to that point. Once you determine precisely where you wish to undo, select the command; then *right* click on it and select **Delete** from the drop-down menu. This will delete all the actions performed up to that command.

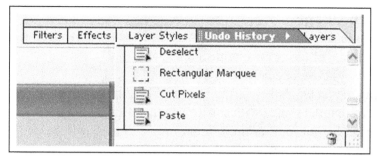

Figure B.3: Undo History

Converting to RGB Mode

The image may need to be changed to **RGB** (Red, Green, Blue) mode in order to color it.
Select **Image > Mode > RGB**. (If the image was imported as a Bitmap, it will need to be first saved as a grayscale image before this step by selecting **Image > Mode > Grayscale**. When the *Grayscale* dialog box appears, retain the size ratio as 1 and press **OK**.)

- If the image needs to be straightened, select **Image > Rotate > Straighten Image**. If this process does not work out satisfactorily, select **Edit > Step Backward** or **Ctrl + Z** to undo and then "manually" rotate the image by going to **Image > Rotate > Custom**; then rotate the image by individual degrees to the left or to the right.
- To sharpen the image, select **Enhance > Adjust Brightness/Contrast > Brightness and Contrast**. In the *Brightness/Contrast* window, use the "sliders" under *Brightness* and *Contrast* to find the optimum settings and press **OK**.

Separating Individual Images from a Scanned Page

1. Select the **Rectangular Marquee** tool from the *Toolbox*. The cursor will turn into a plus sign. Position the cursor above one corner of the image and drag the rectangle across the image so that the moving dashes surround the image. (Tip: To redo the marquee, click onto the gray border around the image and select the **Rectangular Marquee** tool again.)
2. Select **Edit > Copy** or **Ctrl + C** on the keyboard to copy the image.
3. Choose **File > New** or **Ctrl + N** to create a separate new file. The *New* dialog box will appear. Give the file a short descriptive name and select **Transparent** under *Contents*; then press **OK**. 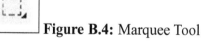**Figure B.4:** Marquee Tool
4. To copy the image onto the new file, select **Edit > Paste** or **Ctrl + V**.
5. Press on the **Maximize** button on the top-right corner of the workspace. A gray border will surround the image.

Trimming an Image

Select the **Crop** tool from the *Toolbox*.

 Figure B.5: Crop Tool

The cursor will turn into a crop sign. Position the cursor above one corner of the image and drag the rectangle across the image. When the mouse is released, moving dashes will surround the image with square handles. Drag the square handles inward or outward to frame the image as desired. Trimming the image will reduce the size of the file and will cut out any unnecessary elements surrounding the picture.

Creating a Transparent Background

When opening a new image (**File > New**), make sure the transparent box is selected in the opening dialog box.

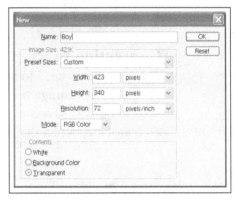

Click on the **Magic Wand** tool and then press on the white background of the image.

Press **Delete** to create a transparent background. Deselect the background by clicking onto the gray area outside of the image. The marching lines will stop. Don't worry if any of the inside areas of the image become transparent. This means that the area is not totally comprised of closed lines or figures; it will need to be closed before adding "fill colors" to the image.

Figure B.6: New Dialog Box

 Figure B.7: Magic Wand Tool

Coloring the Image

Click on the **Paint Bucket** tool and press the **Foreground** color (top square in the icon) to bring up the *Color Picker*.

 Figure B.8: Foreground/Background

There are two main ways to select a color: type in the RGB numbers or use the color slider to select a color field and then click into the main window to select a particular color. Click on *Only Web Colors* to select colors that are safe for the Web. Click in any area of the image to fill the area with color.

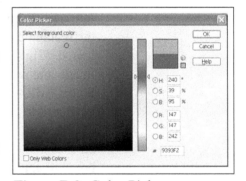

■ To match a color on an image, click on the **Eye Dropper** tool and then click onto a color on the image. The *Foreground* color will change to match the color selected.

Figure B.9: Color Picker

 Figure B.10: Eye Dropper Tool

- To fill in small patches of color, magnify the area by selecting **View > Zoom In** (**Ctrl** key and the **Plus sign** on the keyboard) or **View > Zoom Out** (**Ctrl** and **Minus** sign). (Troubleshooting Tip: If the fill color fills more than just the desired areas, there may be holes in the outline that need to be closed. Change the **Foreground** color to match the outline (black or gray) and click on the **Pencil** tool. Magnify the area you wish to touch up. If the pencil is too wide or too narrow, click on the down arrow next to the pencil size (top left of screen) and select the desired number of pixels using the pop-up slider. Fill in the gaps using the pencil cursor.)

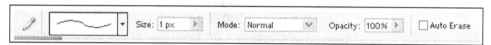

Figure B.11: Pencil Options

- To erase undesirable marks or lines, click on the **Eraser** tool. Choose an eraser tool from the eraser options; then hold and drag the cursor over the marks to erase.

Figure B.12: Eraser Options

Resizing the Image

Select **Image > Resize > Image Size**. Be sure *Constrain Proportions* is checked; then change the height or width. The resolution of an image (number of pixels per inch) can also be changed. Select 72 for images that will be shown on the Web, 300 for black and white images in print, and 600 for printed color images. A higher resolution increases the image quality, but subsequently requires more memory to store. To change the size of the canvas (the background of the image), select **Image > Resize > Canvas Size**.

Saving the Image

Select **File > Save As**. In the *Save In* dialog box, navigate to the *image* folder previously created on the Desktop. Be sure to give your file a descriptive name and select .gif for black and white or colored drawings or .bmp for colored photos.

Bibliography

Bruner, J.S. (1990). *Acts of Meaning*. Cambridge, Massachusetts: Harvard University Press.

Kistler, M. (1988). *Draw Squad*. Simon & Schuster: New York.

Lambert, J. (2002). Digital Storytelling: *Capturing Lives, Creating Community*. Berkeley, CA: Digital Diner Press.

Lambert, J. & Mullen, N. (2002). *Digital Storytelling Cookbook and Travelling Companion* (version 3.6). Berkeley, CA: Center for Digital Storytelling.

Levin, J.R. (1993). Mnemonic strategies and classroom learning: A 20-year report card. *Elementary School Journal, 94*, 235–244.

Schank, R.C. (1990). *Tell Me a Story: Narrative and Intelligence*. Evanston, Illinois: Northwestern University Press.

Williams, R. (1994). *The Non-Designer's Design Book*. Peachpit Press: Berkeley, CA.

Index

R

S

T

W

About the Authors

Dusti D. Howell has a Ph.D. in curriculum and instruction with an emphasis in educational communications and technology and a Ph.D. minor in educational psychology from the University of Wisconsin, Madison. He is an Associate Professor in the Instructional Design and Technology Department at Emporia State University. In addition to digital storytelling, his expertise includes high-tech study skills and digital learning strategies. He has taught at every grade level from first through graduate school. Dusti is a frequent speaker at state and national meetings and conferences and enjoys conducting workshops and professional development seminars.

Deanne K. Howell teaches professional development courses and workshops. She currently teaches online courses for Emporia State University, including the very popular Powerful PowerPoint for Educators. Deanne holds a Masters degree in Curriculum and Instruction from the University of Wisconsin, Madison. She has taught in public, private, and international schools.

Dusti and Deanne are authors of several books on technological applications in the classroom and vocabulary acquisition. They lead SolidA, Inc., a high tech study skills and digital learning company that teaches and motivates students to perform at their highest level. They can be reached at stories@solida.net.